I0417148

Willful Evolution

The Path to Advanced Cognitive Awareness and a Personal Shift in Consciousness

by
Endall Beall

Copyright © 2015 Endall Beall
All rights reserved.
ISBN-13: 978-1512098259

DEDICATION

This book is dedicated to all true seekers of higher consciousness.

Table of Contents

ACKNOWLEDGMENTS

I want to acknowledge all the researchers into matters spiritual over the ages, whether they ever understood what they were seeking or not. Their attempts to pierce the veil of human cognition has kept the quest alive long enough for others to succeed in their own quest for understanding.

I wish to thank Richard Redhawk for his contribution of the cover art for this book.

Prologue

This book is not a philosophy, nor is it about philosophy. This book will be perceived as a philosophy by most readers for the simple reason that they do not yet have the cognitive ability to see beyond their own thinking processes to comprehend it as more than philosophy. This is not to deride you, the reader, but is instead an invitation to understand a greater part of yourself that you have yet to comprehend.

The human species has spent tens of thousands of years making the same historical mistakes over and over again due to the simple factor of their limited system of cognition. Our religions as well as our political systems are all governed with a top down mentality of perception. As a general rule, most of us operate from the standpoint of believing that some person or god-like entity is in control of our lives, has greater wisdom and greater insight than ourselves, and we all accept this premise to be generally true. This concept is one of accepted subservience.

This book is about advancing human conscious awareness. It is not about philosophy, nor is it the wild meanderings of some malcontent trying to set themselves up as the next guru. This book is about *you* and what is required to *advance your own conscious awareness.*

There are numerous studies into consciousness being conducted virtually all the time. Some of these studies are being done by physicists like Bernardo Kastrup. Others have been done in the past by psychologists like Carl Jung, or philosophers like Friedrich Nietzsche and many others over the past few thousand years. The ones who are most adept at describing their own adventures into advanced cognition are generally deemed as philosophers by the general public for the simple reason that the average human being does not have the correct cognitive measuring tools to comprehend the ideas that these forerunners of consciousness often possess. Therefore all such presentations are considered philosophical in their nature. Often times, such presentations *are* philosophical when the person putting forth their ideas on consciousness has not yet advanced into a different, higher level form of cognitive awareness. Saying this does not in any way diminish what they are trying to achieve by investigating the origin of consciousness. It merely means that they have not yet evolved into a different system of cognitive awareness to comprehend what they are seeking to unravel.

As a species, we all comprehend reality as we perceive it. This perception is limited by rules established by our ancestors and our presumed authorities who dictate to all of us from birth what reality is and is not. In all fairness, they were also indoctrinated in the same manner you were, by their own parents and peers, and their own presumed authority figures. As a result of us having to accept the definitions passed down to us by our predecessors, and they in their turn by the same circumstances, we continue onward with the same system of cognition that everyone agrees must be reality.

This cognitive systems works through societal pressure to continue within the accepted definition of what reality is and is not. It constitutes a form of multi-generational brainwashing from one generation to the next, all designed to maintain the status quo of our current cognitive system. If one does manage to escape this system of cognition, they get classified as a *mystic, guru, shaman* or *Master* of some school of esoteric thought. Yet many of these so-called masters are simply hucksters with something to sell the gullible public. Having the wisdom to determine the real ones from the frauds takes keen discernment which, sadly, our present system of cognition seems to be lacking in great quantity.

In speaking of our cognitive abilities, I am not speaking in regard to intelligence, nor am I speaking in regard to what we call the educational system. A cognitive system has to do with perceptual awareness. One can be the most educated person on the planet and still be constrained by the common cognitive perception of reality shared by the greater mass of humanity. The amount of education, i.e. the collection of facts and formulas, will not alter ones cognitive awareness, nor does advancement in conscious cognitive awareness originate from any source outside of ourselves.

As children virtually all of us were told by our parents that we would understand things better when we grew up. As we matured, what we did not understand as a child became patently evident when we reached adulthood. In like kind, in trying to explain a completely different system of cognition than the one globally in use at this time, one finds themselves in the same position as that adult who told you that you would understand better when you mature. A child does not have the mental framework to fully understand what we can understand as an adult. Operating from the current human cognitive system puts us back in that position of a child who does not have the tools to yet comprehend what is presented when one encounters the concept of a completely different system of cognition.

We have organizations like the Institute for Noetic Sciences (IONS) who are hard at work researching into human consciousness. There are people from many other different fields all researching human consciousness in one form or another, covering everything from studying the mechanics of the brain to more recent research into other forms of human cognitive fields like the heart-mind at the Institute for HeartMath. Millions of people worldwide are searching for a solution to what plagues humanity and its limited consciousness. People are pursuing many different schools of thought - everything from Eastern esotericism, Buddhism, Taoism, mystical aspects of Christianity, Sufism, Theosophy, the New Age and secret societies. Millions of people are searching for some kind of shift in conscious awareness. Unfortunately, most are looking outside themselves for the solutions.

On the other hand, we have material science which is doing its best to define consciousness through understanding the material mechanics of the brain. It is supposed, by certain scientists, that everything can be quantified through the study of matter - i.e. the material world of physicality, or materialism. Quantum physicists are discovering that the restrictive interpretations of material science are insufficient to explain what quantum mathematics is pointing to where reality is concerned, and many of the quantum physicists are doing their own research into consciousness, which has led many of them to turn to ancient and modern spiritual teachings in an attempt to understand what quantum physics is revealing.

It doesn't matter if one believes there will be some global shift in consciousness initiated by some outside source, and it doesn't matter what form that perceived external source may present itself to be according to any individual's perceptual belief system. It doesn't matter if they believe in some god or goddess, or pantheon of gods, whether it will be aliens who initiate this shift on consciousness, or the whether the answer is provided by the latest guru. Millions of people around the planet feel a push for a shift in consciousness, but they all seem to be seeking an answer outside themselves. It is not unlike using the amorphous term *they* when people say. "*They* ought to do something". The answer is always the same. *They* are all of us. *They* are you as an individual, particularly when it comes to altering your own cognitive awareness.

I am not going to spend time quoting presumed modern authorities about consciousness in this body of work, for the simple reason that *there are no current qualified authorities* on the subject of expanded cognitive awareness. The multitudes of researchers into consciousness are all failing in one major area - their interpretations about consciousness are all based in a system that cannot comprehend what they are seeking to understand. In essence, they are all looking at something that is larger than our cognitive perception and trying to make it fit into a smaller box of our current level of cognitive awareness. One can't put 100 pounds of sugar into a 1 pound container no matter how many mathematical theories and calculations they perform. For all intents and purposes, all such researchers are doomed to failure so long as they use the current human system of cognition as their measuring stick. The only way anyone can understand this heightened system of cognitive awareness is to throw out the old system and step into the new one.

We live in a world of duality, where one thing is understood in comparison to something else. We all make our choices in life based on this mode of comparison, yet when it comes to trying to explain a different system of cognitive awareness; we have no point of comparative reference based on our current level of cognition. In other words, we can see no other choice from which to choose when it comes to cognitive awareness, so our world of comparative analogy fails us when we are presented with such an idea. It is unknown territory except to the very few to have trod there and understand the difference.

One of the most misunderstood philosophers of the 19th century was Friedrich Nietzsche when he wrote about his *Ubermensch* (Overman) in *Thus Spake Zarathustra*. Adolph Hitler used Nietzsche's description of the *Ubermensch* and misinterpreted the principle to develop the idea of a Master Race, but Hitler's interpretation was done by a man operating in a limited form of cognitive awareness. Hitler could no more grasp the true nature of Nietzsche's *Ubermensch* than most of the readers of this volume can understand it. But I have taken the task to try and interpret the true meaning of the term *Ubermensch* in order to vindicate Nietzsche's work and remove Hitler's misuse of the term to fulfill his own political and egoistic agenda that led to WW II.

Nietzsche wrote that modern man is simply a rope, a connection between the ape and the *Ubermensch.* He viewed mankind, with its current 'herd mentality', as simply a developmental stage to the next level of human cognitive awareness. In *Thus Spake Zarathustra*, Nietzsche wrote,

> "*I teach you the overman.* Man is something that shall be overcome. What have you done to overcome him?"

This question, posed by Nietzsche, lies at the very core of the shift in human consciousness, and it is also the question you need to ask yourself if you intend to move into a state of higher cognitive awareness. When Nietzsche states that, *"Man is something that shall be overcome",* he is not referring to some kind of tyrannical overlords taking the place of man, but is instead referring to our current cognitive system and how it must be overcome if we are ever going to evolve into something better.

His next question, *"What have you done to overcome him?"* is the most relevant, for it refers to what *you* as an individual conscious entity are doing to change that within yourself? Until such time that enough people can evolve themselves into this different system of cognition and become the *Ubermensch* themselves, the entire human race will still suffer the indignity of operating under the materialist view of the world and its handicapping perceptual limitations. Until people can start to see a real choice between these two different systems of cognition, the second system of advanced perceptual awareness doesn't exist except as theory or philosophy. The cognitive system of Nietzsche's overman exists, but it is unattainable so long as our species continues to fervently embrace and defend the current, limited system of cognition.

1

The Misconception of Spirit

The biggest problem facing mankind in understanding a system of higher cognitive awareness comes from the species fascination with the supernatural or spiritual. There are a number of spiritual schools that teach that one's conscious advancement is predicated upon their own actions in order to reach a state of *enlightenment*. Unfortunately, most all of these schools of thought, just like religions, paint a picture of the supernatural. They sell the idea of some unified consciousness that guides the universe of which we are all just small participants in some grand overall plan. Even the physicist Bernardo Kastrup, in his books on studying consciousness, falls prey to the concept of some overarching consciousness of which we are all simply 'eddy's' in a larger stream of consciousness. Although not described as such, this is only one small step removed from the idea of some singular god in control of the universe *a la* religion.

Nietzsche wrote in *Thus Spake Zarathustra:*

"All beings so far have created something beyond themselves; and do you want to be the ebb of this great flood and even go back to the beasts rather than overcome man? What is the ape to man? A laughingstock or a painful embarrassment. And man shall be just that for the overman: a laughingstock or a painful embarrassment. You have made your way from worm to man, and much in you is still worm. Once you were apes, and even now, too, man is more ape than any ape."

Nietzsche's observation is a matter of truth where human consciousness is concerned. The vast majority of humanity still continues to look outside themselves to solve their problems. They manufacture gods, follow gurus, and plead for the aliens to come save us from ourselves, or through science, seek the unified field theory to explain everything for them. All it takes is a view of known history to discover that where consciousness is concerned, we are little removed from our ancestors. Granted, there may be intellectual and technological advancements compared to 2,000 years ago, but the cognitive system of governments today is not that far removed from the governance of the Roman Republic and its subsequent devolution into tyranny under the Caesars. So we have to ask ourselves, have we really evolved where consciousness is concerned? The answer is a deafening "No!"

We have been taught through multiple generations of societal and religious programming to look outside ourselves for answers. We give up our responsibility to be personally accountable to politicians, priests, gurus and any other form of authority so we can all be left alone to pursue our own selfish goals in life. "God gives" and the "Devil made me do it" are the watchwords of global blame. The other end of the spectrum is where lie the Atheists, who believe in nothing but the efforts of man - all necessarily interpreted by the current system of limited cognition and material science.

Millions of people worldwide are still falling for the belief in some form of cosmic Oneness. They believe that there is something like a gigantic hive mind of which we are all just individual parts experiencing our lives so the greater singular consciousness can learn about itself. This belief in some singular master consciousness is as misdirected as the belief in some anthropomorphic God who rules the universe, and even looking at the concept of a God as 'ruler' specifically shows the mindset of billions of humans on this planet who have the psychological need to be ruled over. It is simply the relinquishment of personal responsibility on the largest scale imaginable. Too many people believe that it is some overarching form of consciousness guiding the universe, or some God or another who is at the helm of all creation. We are never responsible for our own actions, our own evolution; it is always someone or something outside ourselves that must do it for us. This is the greatest fallacy that humankind on this planet has ever adopted and it is also our greatest failing characteristic as a species.

I am going on an assumption that most of the preliminary readers of this volume are involved in some manner on some kind of spiritual quest or another. At least that type of individual is seeking more, even if they are unsure what that 'more' is or how they are going to achieve it. Many people are seeking external forms of alleged salvation, seeking messiahs or aliens to save them from the idiocy of humanity. Concepts such as Rapture or some kind of Ascension lure the dependent follower down a road that leads nowhere. There is actually little difference between the two concepts except in the framework of how they are sold. If you are a spiritual seeker who has adopted that wish for Ascension to some other higher-dimensional realm as a type of escape, I can only ask that you recognize the similarity in the concepts. In regard to seeking the supernatural, Nietzsche wrote in *Thus Spake Zarathustra:*

"Behold, I teach you the overman. The overman is the meaning of the earth. Let your will say: the overman *shall be* the meaning of the earth! I beseech you, my brothers, *remain faithful to the earth*, and do not believe those who speak to you of otherworldly hopes! Poison-mixers are they, whether they know it or not. Despisers of life are they, decaying and poisoned themselves, of whom the earth is weary: so let them go."

Nietzsche's detractors call such concepts anti-Christian, but in the modern world, with the pop New Age culture, the same concept applies to all those who seek to exit Earth for some illusion of Ascension, or for aliens coming to whisk them away to some form of technological-spiritual Nirvana. All of it, Rapture, Ascension or alien intervention, is simply a concept of ultimate escapism. No one wants to take responsibility to change themselves, so they seek outside, supernatural forces to do the work for them. It is the pinnacle of spiritual laziness.

20

Because of generations of programming us into our current state of cognitive awareness we have all fallen prey to the concept of spirit being something supernatural. What I want the reader to take away from this presentation is the fact that it only *seems* to be supernatural from the standpoint of our limited awareness. If such a state of consciousness exists and can be perceived by certain individuals, why can't we just as readily accept the idea that what we consider to be supernatural is only a part of a natural process that we simply don't yet understand? Why do we as a species have to elevate such experiences, or tales of spiritual happenings, to a supernatural realm outside ourselves? If such experiences exist, they are part of a natural order of things that our current system of cognition simply denies because understanding it is presently inaccessible to the masses of humanity.

We have to ask ourselves why we elevate those who have accessed this greater river of cognitive awareness as philosophers, gurus or holy men rather than seeking it ourselves without all the supernatural hoopla. If they achieved such levels of cognitive awareness, then why should we believe that we can't do the same thing? Are they not as human as we are? And if we admit that they are human, why do we choose to elevate these men and women to near deified positions rather than choosing to elevate ourselves in like kind? To achieve such a goal will not be found by making one's self subservient, and elevating others who have attained what we believe are perceptually unattainable goals above ourselves. When we elevate others above ourselves, whether gods or men, we make ourselves subservient. Unfortunately, subservience is the framework of the primary cognitive system into which we have all been indoctrinated. To become the overman, we have to reject this mindset in order to advance our cognitive awareness.

To advance into what people call spiritual understanding, or the second cognition, we have to strip it of all concepts of the supernatural. We also have to strip ourselves of embracing such limiting and subservient concepts that only saints or holy men can achieve it, and this requires advancing beyond what our current level of cognitive awareness presents us with. With a mindset of subservience of any kind, we can never advance into a cosmic realm of equal conscious opportunity. You can never be equal so long as you think you are lesser than anything or anyone else. You will always be a lesser being for the simple reason that you believe such a thing to be true.

What some call the spirit path is basically a willful choice to evolve yourself to the point where you surpass the limitations of our current thinking processes as a species. As Nietzsche wrote, to view humanity from the perspective of the overman, humanity as it currently operates is either laughable or a painful embarrassment. All we have to do is look at human behavior to see that we are a painfully embarrassing species, what with our wars and dramas, territorial and religious imperatives coupled with greed and control. If one takes a seriously objective look at modern mankind, there are very few redeemable qualities overall that we should continue to embrace, yet our species has done the same things over and over again for millennia. Technology and science have not advanced our collective consciousness one whit in the last 10,000 years. So where does the solution lie? It lies within each individual to recognize that as a species we are just not getting it, and it relies on the individual to change themselves and their cognitive awareness in the face of such limited perceptual abilities. What I am talking about is a form of *willful evolution*, and it is the only way that you can move up from the simple cognitive system that currently controls your mind into a greater cognitive awareness. If you want to see the overman, you have to turn yourself into that being. In John 16:33, the words attributed to Jesus put it this way:

> *"These things I have spoken to you, so that in Me you may have peace. In the world you have tribulation, but take courage; I have overcome the world."*

What this passage is relating is no different than what Nietzsche wrote about man overcoming man. When Jesus says that he has "overcome the world" he is specifically stating that he has moved from the limited cognition of humanity into a higher level of cognitive awareness. In its simplest form he is telling us that if he could do it, so can we. Further, in John 14:12 Jesus stated:

> *"Truly, truly, I say to you, he who believes in Me, the works that I do, he will do also; and greater works than these he will do; because I go to the Father.*

Once again, Jesus is revealing a cognitive truth, not a message of religious devotion. Simply stated in modern English, he is saying that if you believe in what I have done, through the process I used, you will do the same things and even more. The additional phrase about going to the Father is most likely a later addition by the Bible editors designed to sell the concept of God, rather than being part of the original message itself.

Humans operate from the five primary senses. Anything that goes beyond these sensory tools is considered to be somehow supernatural. Many people can accept that some of us have psychic abilities, but we still relegate the concept to the supernatural. So long as we continue to see such abilities as 'gifts from god' or whatever, we will never develop the sensory capability to experience them ourselves. The five primary senses are our current measure of *reality*. Anything that goes beyond these five senses is considered 'extrasensory perception' or supernatural. Yet we once again have to ask ourselves if such abilities are in fact extrasensory, or more aptly a form of sensing things beyond the limited material framework of the five senses that define our strictly material perception of the world, are they really extrasensory, or are they simply *additional* senses that we have yet to embrace?

I have stated that trying to understand spirit, or advanced cognitive awareness, cannot be generally perceived using the tools of the materialistic form of measure. If we restrict ourselves to the belief that all there is can be found through the primary five senses, and believe that anything that goes beyond the limited sensory perception of those five senses must be somehow supernatural, are we not then handicapping ourselves by our own disbelief? Are we not denying the possibility that such talents exist in ourselves because our primary measuring stick *is* our primary five senses? And if we all do have the latent sensory capability to tap into more than what the primary five senses present to us, then how do we tap into it? The answer lies in our personal belief structures. If we do not believe we can do such things, that they are unimaginable or unattainable, then we are doomed to failure to ever tap into such skills inherent in our nature.

It is not belief in these presumed supernatural abilities that will bring us access to such talents. Beliefs are insufficient to make things happen. Belief is simply a wish that something is true, and as such, belief will lead one nowhere. But if one sees the possibility and works to remove the perceptual barriers that keep us from reaching for such presumed 'supernatural' abilities, then possibilities open up for our conscious advancement. Disbelief is a greater inhibitor to one's conscious development than accepting that such things are possible.

What most people consider to be spiritual happenings, whether through religious dogma or other spiritual teachings, fall into the category of being supernatural or unearthly. By believing spirit to be supernatural, we limit our own capabilities by making myth out of an alternative truth. There is no such thing as the supernatural or paranormal. Both terms denote what we consider natural or normal. From the platform of our current cognitive system, we see these abilities as something outside ourselves, and the only explanations we can give for such abilities is mystical or supernatural. We use our primary five senses as our measure of nature and normalcy. If our five senses are the tool of measure for what is natural or normal, then even if we do possess a 6th or 7th sense, it would not be considered natural or normal by those standards of measurement.

The point I am putting forth for your consideration is the fact that our five 'normal' senses are insufficient to measure any other sensory capabilities that go beyond that norm without classifying them as somehow mystical or supernatural. If they are latent capabilities, how can they be remotely supernatural, except in the manner of our limited thinking processes and our system of measuring 'normalcy'? To become Nietzsche's overman, we have to acknowledge that these purported supernatural abilities are in fact a natural aspect of our cognitive capabilities that are simply as yet untapped. So then, are they really supernatural at all, or does our limited belief and current cognitive system of normality simply limit us in our own latent perceptual abilities?

This is the simplest set of examples I can provide to show that our current system of cognition is incapable of comprehending a higher level of cognitive awareness. All the measuring tools for understanding such a different system of cognitive perception do not exist in the current framework, and as such, trying to explain it will always fall short when we use the measuring stick available of presumed 'normalcy' to comprehend something longer than that stick. We can imagine sort of what that system might be like, but ultimately, the conclusions are always reached by that same limited system of cognitive measure in any attempt to define it, and it always comes up with the mystical solution.

We have no shortage of science fiction, fantasy films and books that intimate such abilities, and in virtually all cases, the final interpretation falls into categories of limited human consciousness. One who finds power usually winds up abusing it to the detriment of mankind, or they are portrayed as some sort of messiah figure. You rarely, if ever, see one who gets to be enlightened or more advanced in consciousness that is not portrayed in these manners. The current cognitive system can't perceive such an individual ever becoming anything different than either a threat or a savior. Both portrayals should stand as stark evidence of our limited cognition at this point of our conscious evolution.

The current cognitive system is driven by either paranoia or wishful escapism; fear or fantasy. The truth lies somewhere in between, but our current system of cognition can't see beyond this simple duality of choices. We are bombarded through the media with the ideas of ego-driven hero figures with superpowers, or with the mass paranoia of societies that fear anyone and anything that goes beyond their limited perceptual capabilities. Humans on one hand crave change for the better, but on the other hand fear making such changes, for any person with extraordinary, supernatural powers or abilities is perceived to be a threat to changing or harming them. They are caught in this duality and can see no third alternative which will present the way out of this cognitive morass. Humanity is caught in a mental trap from which the current system of cognition offers no solutions, and they are all vehemently defending the current cognitive system because they see no alternative to what they know. In this regard, all of humanity is enslaved to this limited cognitive system and lacks the imagination to see any real alternative unless it is packaged in the wrapper of supernaturalism.

27

Let me take this opportunity to paint an alternative picture to the standard narrative we have all come to accept as illustrated above. Imagine if you can a person who has moved into a different level of cognitive awareness, who has outgrown what it currently means to be a 'normal' human in their cognitive capabilities. But rather than turning into some kind of egotistical superhero or threat to humanity as some kind of super villain, this person chooses instead to try and lead others into the same level of cognitive awareness. This person is not a leader as the current system portrays them as some sort of guru, but is more of a guide, working to try and wake people up so they could all enjoy the benefits of advanced cognitive abilities.

In many respects, this is what so many enlightened individuals throughout the ages have attempted to do, yet what they failed to take into consideration is the lack of perceptual ability with the *normal* system of human cognition to understand what they have been trying to relate to the public. Many philosophers and spiritual teachers have tried over and over again to explain a different system of conscious awareness, yet I find that none of them have addressed the problem of us facing two different systems of cognition - except for one teacher - the Yaqui shaman Don Juan Matús. He explained in no uncertain terms that in order to understand spirit (higher cognitive awareness), we have to recognize that we are talking about *two different systems of cognition.* On the primary level of normal human cognitive abilities, we do not have the tools to perceive the second level of cognition, yet from the second, higher level of cognitive awareness, one can see both systems.

28

The bad thing about the Don Juan teachings is that their presentation was left to an individual operating totally in the same primary cognitive system as the rest of humanity, and the messenger therefore misinterpreted what he was taught through his total lack of comprehension and garbled the message through his own profound ignorance. This is no different than scholars trying to interpret the works of certain philosophers and teachers based on one cognitive system lacking understanding of the other. When one operating from the normal system of cognition receives the teachings of one like Buddha, Lao Tzu, or Jesus, institutionalized religious organizations are always the result. The complete lack of comprehension of what the followers are being shown is lost because the tools of measurement for that comprehension are completely different.

Many members of humanity on this planet want something different, something better, but for the most part what they are seeking has not been aptly explained without the introduction of mystical twaddle by the spiritual hucksters or the lack of appropriate tools for interpretation from other researchers. Everyone either wants to mystify it or measure it, and no matter which of the two options is used, the common interpretive factor is the primary cognitive system called 'normal'.

The term *expanded awareness* means exactly that. It means to expand your awareness beyond what it currently is. It doesn't mean take larger principles of awareness or cognition you may be presented with and try to squeeze them into the smaller box of your current perceptual awareness. It is an invitation to move beyond such limitations into something more than you currently perceive. You will never understand how to use a sixth sense if you are only using five senses by which to measure it. To expand your perceptual awareness, you have to expand yourself. You can't expand your cognitive awareness and rigidly maintain the status quo of the current perceptual paradigm at the same time and expect to advance. To do so is profoundly counterproductive to what you are seeking to achieve. You would be working at cross-purposes. It is like wanting to have your cake and eat it too. It can't be done.

If you are genuinely seeking to understand higher levels of conscious awareness, you are going to have to pave the way there for yourself. Sitting at the feet of some mystical guru, or waiting on science to explain it all to you will not move you one inch forward in what you seek to understand. But at least, at this point, you have been shown that you are seeking a completely different type of cognitive awareness than you currently know, and it has absolutely nothing to do with supernaturalism, mysticism or some kind of presumed holiness. That critical piece of information in itself may clarify just where your so-called spirit path is ultimately leading you. Nietzsche put it this way in *Thus Spake Zarathustra:*

"Man is a rope, tied between beast and overman - a rope over an abyss. A dangerous across, a dangerous on-the-way, a dangerous looking-back, a dangerous shuddering and stopping.
"What is great in man is that he is a bridge and not an end: what can be loved in man is that he is an *overture* and a *going under*.
"I love those who do not know how to live, except by going under, for they are those who cross over."

We are at a crossroad for human consciousness. In that respect, we are walking that rope over the abyss. We are the connecting thread between who we currently are as a species and who we want to be. This path to conscious advancement, as Nietzsche accurately portrays, is a dangerous path. To step into higher level awareness, each of us must *"go under"*, which doesn't mean to die a physical death, but amounts to the death of the ego and the limited system of cognitive awareness in which the ego thrives. As Nietzsche says in the last sentence, the only ones who will cross over to this different level of cognition are the ones who will destroy their current system of cognition governed by the ego. As don Juan taught Carlos Castenada, *"I want to see your person die, not your body."* In different words from two separate teachers we are told that in order to move into a higher level of cognitive awareness, the current system of the ego personality must die or 'go under'.

2

Expanded Possibilities

Humanity in general seems to make the same perceptual mistakes no matter the venue of spiritual teachings. From the time of the spiritualist movement in the mid-1800's up to the time of Madame Helena Blavatsky creating her own version of spirituality through the development of her dogma of Theosophy, the modern pop New Age spiritual movement can be tracked back to its origins. The modern spiritual movement is rife with angels, aliens, Ascended Masters and a host of purportedly long-dead channeled entities pleading with humanity to follow their words. The problem is that the words of these so-called channeled entities lead nowhere. It is all a carrot and stick approach to understanding spirit through mystical hogwash, with no shortage of lures to play upon the ego personality seeking spiritual or magical powers for all the wrong reasons, and a real shortage of factual and usable information through which one can truly advance their own awareness. It is still dangling the carrot of the supernatural or the mystical as the path to enlightenment.

After decades of personal research into matters of spirit I can testify to the validity of what I just wrote. The pop New Age movement is no different than religions selling salvation or heavenly reward. Both venues, religion and the New Age movement, are long on selling dreams and mystical fantasies and both fall far short of telling anyone how to achieve any real perceptual advancement. They are selling their followers dogmas, a bill of goods. Religions want you in their temples or mosques praying and paying tithes, and living by their religious mandates, while the New Age gurus get their tithes by selling books and doing national and international seminars. All of them are selling some sort of salvation in a different format, yet few if any of these so-called spiritual leaders can tell you squat about personal development beyond telling you to pray or to meditate. There is an abysmal void in both venues for providing any real tools to advance one's self. The fact is, they are not interested in your advancement, they are interested in your money and your elevating their egos onto pedestals so you can grovel at their feet for forgiveness or enlightenment. The sad commentary about the present cognitive system governed by crude ego desires is that so few are willing to call the con game for what it is. By the billions we flock in droves to the temples of idiocy groveling at the feet of some God or guru, seeking someone who will just make it alright for us lowly human followers.

In general, these followers are all seeking that golden ticket to heaven or Nirvana, and most are willing to pay any fee to get there. Few, if any, of these adherents are willing to do the real work required to fix their lives, for that would mean taking responsibility for one's own actions. This, the ego will never do.

In general, for there are a few exceptions, the greater mass of humanity lives in a world governed and controlled by the ego personality. Under the control of this ego personality, everyone is the center of their own universe. No one looks at anything beyond how it affects them personally. In this aspect, every human on this planet is self-centered and self-indulgent. Even those who are doing humanitarian work, for the most part, are self-serving because they have the bragging rights of being compassionate and caring about humanity. Virtually everyone on this planet is self-serving in that regard, and no matter the compassionate front they present to society, they are still at the center of their own universe. Their ego feels elevated because they are exhibiting such compassion.

Everyone is either a victor or a victim in the mentality of the ego. The ego part of ourselves thrives on drama. If we view the world objectively, it is simply a magnified example of the ego on a larger scale. Our governments, religions and businesses are all simply an expanded expression of the ego personality. Every nation is self-centered, every religion is elitist and equally self-centered, selling their doctrines as the one true way in opposition to all other religions who are equally professing their way as the one true way. If we compare our global institutions to the self-centeredness of the individual, we all see a reflection of the ego personality. Everyone wants their piece of the pie and damned be everyone else.

We all sit around and blast everyone else for their shortcomings, but how many of you have actually looked at yourself and your own shortcomings? Have you ever decided to quit laying blame on others and accept responsibility for your own actions of a similar nature first? Until you are willing to do this, you will never step into that second level of cognitive awareness, for you are as short-sighted as the rest of humanity and as equally selfish and ruled by your own ego as they are. So long as you neglect to find and correct the faults in yourself while castigating others for the same faults, you are part of the problem, not part of the solution.

People join social networks seeking *like-minded* individuals. Have you ever wondered why people prefer others who think like them rather than people who don't think like them, who may actually teach them something different rather than people who solidify their own ego belief structure through only like-minded interchanges? The only way you are going to advance your cognitive awareness is to learn other perspectives. In doing so you are going to find out that your perception of the real world is nothing but a fantasy world made up and enforced by your own ego, continually seeking like-minded people to reinforce your own perceptual illusions.

In seeking internal critical analysis of one's own shortcomings, you are not going to fix yourself by saying affirmations day in and day out. Reciting affirmations is nothing more than the hope that by continued uttering of positive affirmations you will fix what is wrong with you. In essence, it is you lying to yourself to convince yourself that you are something you want to be, not something that you are. Affirmations will not lead you to a different awareness. It may alter some of your ego's habits if done long enough, if you lie to yourself hard enough, but it is not going to alter your perceptual awareness. Your ego self will still be in charge of your life. Affirmations are nothing more than a personalized form of behavioral modification within the first system of cognitive awareness.

In order to move into a *real* shift in consciousness, we have to *expand beyond* the current system of cognition. There are a number of readers here that hope for that shift of consciousness, but how many of you have ever considered what you are trying to shift away *from?* It makes no difference that one has a desire for a shift in consciousness *to* something different if they have no idea the consciousness they are trying to shift away *from*. You can't know where you are going until you know where you are. Where we are, and have been for thousands of years, is the consciousness of an ego-oriented world. So long as we let the ego rule our consciousness, our world will be only a reflection of our own egos on a cultural scale, and unfortunately, that is where humanity finds itself to this day.

Buddhism teaches about transcending the ego. Don Juan Matús called it the death of your person. Nietzsche called it walking the rope of man to the overman. It matters not the terminology used, it all amounts to the same core principle. In order to transcend into a new level of cognitive awareness, we have to know what the old one is. The current system of ego cognition is our curse and also our greatest impediment to evolutionary conscious advancement. I have explained that there are two different systems of cognition and how one can see the other, but the primary can't see the secondary level of cognitive awareness. From that secondary level of cognition, Nietzsche put it this way in *Thus Spake Zarathustra:*

> *"I no longer feel in common with you; the very cloud which I see beneath me, the blackness and heaviness at which I laugh—that is your thunder-cloud."*

From the standpoint of an ego personality, this observation will only appear as someone arrogant looking down on you. Yet arrogance is not what Nietzsche is relating to when making this observation. It is a testament to his own cognitive advancement. When one advances into the second level of cognition, they no longer have the same cognitive perception in common with people who are still ruled by their egos. From the second cognitive level, the world of the ego *is* filled with the blackness and heaviness he describes.

Admittedly, he is looking *down* at this thunder-cloud, but it is not from a standpoint of ego superiority. It is an observation from a higher level of cognition than humanity currently operates. When one can comprehend this perspective, then they can see that there is in fact a higher level of cognitive abilities that can see the absolute fruitlessness of the ego world. The ego world is filled with turmoil at all levels - that blackness and heaviness. We all have to scramble to simply put food on the table under this cognitive system. We are all operating at some level of slavery, and the mental slavery of the ego is the most dastardly tyranny under which any of us can live. As Nietzsche relates in the sentence following the last passage:

37

"Ye look aloft when ye long for exaltation; and I look downward because I am exalted."

When Nietzsche makes this statement, once again it is not from ego arrogance, but simply a statement of fact. The ego part of all of us seeks external validation at all levels, even looking to the heavens for exaltation, without ever realizing that being exalted resides in all of us as potential. The word exalted can be interpreted in two different ways - first, as a person of rank or high status held in high regard, which is the most common interpretation - secondly, it is a state of extreme happiness. For his comments about the ability to laugh at the dark cloud, I would suggest that Nietzsche was exalted and happy that he had escaped and transcended the tyranny of the ego world. I have that same happiness, but it is not the same type of emotional giddiness as expressed by the ego personality in all people as happiness. It is a happiness of accomplishment, of having crossed the abyss of ego insantity into a world more sane than that of the ego.

This different cognitive world opens doors of perception that our five senses don't normally perceive. Once one fully crosses over, they can see the limitations of the 'real world' as supported and defended by the ego personality. I do not laugh at the darkness of the ego world. Rather, I would see other people step out of it into a new evolutionary cycle of consciousness. We can never hope to change the world around us if we don't have the strength to change ourselves. When push comes to shove, the only person we have any actual control over is ourselves, and under the rule of the ego, even that control is a tenuous affair.

Under the spell of the ego program, our minds are not our own. The move into understanding spirit comes when one removes the influence and control of their own egos. Buried beneath all the ego illusions you will find the real you - the Self that you actually are, absent the influencing factors of your own ego prison guard. The spirit quest, if one wants to call it that, is a quest for awareness of who you are in your core essence. The ego is an overlaid personality onto your true self. The ego personality is shaped and programmed by our parents, our peers, our cultures, our religions, political ideologies and our schools. If one were to remove all these programmed aspects that make up our egos, then one will find their true self underneath it all.

Through multitudes of generations we have all been hopelessly brainwashed into what we accept as reality. Everything we think is perceptually real is simply a programmed illusion, enforced by societal and peer pressure to keep us all coloring within the lines of accepted cultural perceptual norms. If you look at psychology and psychiatry, they are not really interested in healing the psyche, but are more interested in making people *well* enough to function within the acceptable perceptual norms of their society.

To turn into the overman, to step into that second level of cognitive awareness, what we perceive as our reality must be challenged. This is not to say that we do not feel pain when we bang our shin against the coffee table, it means that what we *perceive* to be real is the illusion. All of human history has been tainted by the hands of the victors. All spiritual teachings have been tainted by those who either did not understand the teachings or who misinterpreted the meaning based on their own limited cognition.

The teachings of Socrates, Buddha, Don Juan, Jesus and Nietzsche have all been misinterpreted by people operating in the primary human cognitive system. We are left with the interpretations of speculators as to their meanings. We follow the teachings of those who came afterwards, who turned spiritual teachings either into philosophy, mysticism or religion - none of which can reliably guide us to that next level of evolutionary cognitive advancement.

Evolution is a fact of life, although I feel that Darwin's theory of evolution is off the mark. There are two forms of evolutionary factors which I ask the reader to consider. The first form of evolution has to do with species' adapting due to environmental circumstances that make staying the same untenable. This is evolution as a mandate through external adaptation. The other type of evolution that you will never see discussed in the context of consciousness studies is what I call *willful evolution*. Advancing cognitive awareness will likely never develop under environmental adaptive evolution. It takes willful evolution to advance one's own consciousness. Willful evolution is based on the internal drive to transcend the level of consciousness at which humans currently operate. Willful evolution occurs by personal choice. The spirit path is an individual path. It is not done within group environments like churches or political parties. The spirit path, for those with the most dedicated desire to succeed through their own efforts, is willful evolution. It is only through willful evolution that one will transcend into the second cognition.

This advancement will not come about through wishful thinking, beliefs, simple affirmations, or praying incessantly to some god to make it happen for you. It will not happen no matter how fervently you believe that something external will bring it to you. You are individually and totally responsible for making this take place within yourself. It takes focus and full time dedication. You will never succeed by simply providing lip service or expressing the wish that it happens for you. It is a discipline that is not given away freely. There is an admission cost to second cognition, you have to work for it - it has to be earned. This is why it has been reserved for only the most dedicated members of humanity throughout the ages. This is not an expression of an elitist mindset, for the opportunity is there for everyone. The greatest problem is that humanity is too lazy to do the work required to make it happen overall. It is this inherent laziness that leads us to the crossroad we find ourselves at today, desiring a shift in consciousness but being too lazy as individuals to make it a reality.

<u>3</u>

<u>The Argument against Oneness</u>

Many people worldwide are hooked on the idea of a singular God or a single overarching consciousness that is some kind of presumed master of the universe as touched on previously. This concept is one of the most handicapping of all human belief systems, and it is exactly that, a system of belief. One has to ask that if there were some primary guiding principle in the universe, why does it just sit idly aside and let all this idiocy that surrounds us continue? If it exists and is so presumably wise, why hasn't it learned from the mistakes of humanity yet and corrected its error?

Many people hold the mistaken impression that this singular cosmic intelligence is somehow learning about itself through us, its lowly creations. If one adopts this idea, then they have to face the fact that this entity, god or supreme consciousness, is not in the least bit all knowing or all wise. The concept in itself is contradictory viewed in the harsh light of logic even from our current limited system of cognitive awareness. So we have to ask why so many people from all walks of life still adhere to such a concept?

I propose a new concept for people to consider. The path to higher cognitive awareness is achieved through individual effort, focus and eventually, understanding. If there were some overarching consciousness running this show, we would have to believe that the first time someone became enlightened, this consciousness would have learned from the conscious experience and made adjustments to share the blessings of this new revelation with the rest of its creations. Yet this has never happened, so that leads us to the ultimate conclusion that we are each all on our own. We are each individually in charge of developing our own conscious awareness. It will not be given to us by some benevolent god or creator. If you want it, you have to make it happen.

Examples from humans who attained any degree of enlightenment on this planet make the foregoing observations painfully obvious when you think about it. The few that strive for realization and understanding with an unbending intent, like Buddha, Jesus, Nietzsche or Don Juan, are the ones who reap the benefits of willful evolution on a personal level, while the rest of humanity is left to wallow in the ghettoes of the ego mind.

The ego demands external validation in all its deeds and actions. It craves acknowledgement and, whether good or bad, it craves being noticed. Whether you are the victim or the victor in your own ego self-reflection, you demand that somebody else feeds that self-image. The search for external validation is found through

43

sports, awards, public acclaim and even college degrees that you can hang on your wall to proclaim to all the world who you are - yet none of this is the real you. It is the ego perception that you are feeding within yourself. You are playing the game of your own mental slave master who has convinced you that it is you. The highest form of external recognition is to claim recognition from God! Heck, if God says you're okay (via your religious beliefs), then you must be a wonderful person! At least, so thinks the ego.

When you can see and understand the ego program, then you can start to see your perception of the world around you start to unravel. That is the first step forward into the second cognition. When you can see it in yourself and admit that your ego is no different than anyone else's, then you are really going to get in motion. When you can locate and remove all the aspects within yourself that are actually ego and not your true self, you will be nearing that second level of cognitive awareness. The ego is the enemy of mankind, the enemy of a free consciousness. The only thing that will disagree with this truthful observation is your own ego, who wants to continue to keep your mind enslaved. When you can ultimately see that and remove this poisonous viper from your mind, you will be a new type of human being, operating from a higher level of human cognitive awareness.

If there was a single overarching consciousness in the universe, why hasn't it figured out this simple truth? If it is the all-creator, why did it curse us with the ego program at all? These are not rhetorical or philosophical questions. They are designed as an invitation for you to start doing some serious critical thinking. They are a foundation from which you can launch your challenge to the perceptual illusions hammered into you from childhood - if you have the guts and the desire to succeed.

What the ego part of us fears most is that there is not some ultimate entity at the helm of creation. It shudders at the thought that this might all be a cosmic free-for-all, where every consciousness is ultimately responsible for its own actions, conscious development and its own evolution. I'm here to tell you folks, that's the way it is, and the sooner you accept it the stronger you will be in your resolve to become something better and greater than you are.

Under the control of the ego, Earth humans have a bad form of species arrogance. We consider and measure everything from our inhibited global system of cognition. If we can't recognize the cognitive potential in our own species, we are not fit to deal with other beings from other worlds who may have surpassed our limited understanding. If we can't outgrow the fear of evil aliens wanting to eat your face, or turning them into some kind of gods or saviors, we don't deserve their company. Through the ego part of us, we are scared to death of the vast cosmos, particularly if there is not a singular guiding force to endorse our species stupidity, yet to this day, the options we accept are the options of the extremes of duality thinking - doom or salvation.

The only unity there is anywhere in the universe is through cognizant individuals working with other consciousnesses of advanced cognition for the betterment of their societies without having hidden ego agendas to fulfill along the way. One might call such an attitude altruistic, and from the standpoint of our current cognitive system, this is true. The current perceptual system of humanity is one of distrust for anything foreign or different. We all hate and fear the other. We spend lifetimes running from phantoms created through mass propaganda rather than discovering any difference for ourselves. We embrace controversy and conflict over collaboration and co-operation time and time again, all to the detriment of our individual and species advancement. We are so lazy as a species under the current form of cognitive awareness that we rarely do our own investigative research, and choose instead to let a bunch of paid hacks we call the Press and Academia dictate to us what they think we should think. Unfortunately, most people in their laziness accept these lies and make their decisions based on ego-generated emotional reactions more than any mode of even rational thought.

I hate to say it, but if you look at this species on a global scale, this plague of ignorance is what controls the world. If I were part of an advanced alien race, I wouldn't want to set a foot on this planet of continual ego insanity out of fear of catching the mental contagion that rules humans. But there is a way out, at least on a personal level, and that is through advancing your own cognitive abilities. Quit relying on any idea that anyone, god or alien, is going to come save us from ourselves. The only savior each and every one of us has looks back at us from the mirror. The sooner you accept this idea, the sooner you can remove your consciousness from the herd mentality of the ego-controlled masses.

Stepping into the higher level of cognition is not an easy thing to do or to live with in our modern world. Once you attain that higher state of cognitive awareness you will finally see the human ego-controlled world for what it is. This may cause you dismay, for you will no longer be part of that herd mentality. You will truly walk alone, unless you are fortunate enough to find others who have made that same transition of consciousness. As Nietzsche wrote, you will no longer have anything in common with them for you will have transcended the mental prison that enslaves the rest of humanity. You are going to have to be strong in the face of such odds. You are still going to have to function in a society that can no more comprehend your state of cognitive awareness any more than they could comprehend the mind of God, if God existed.

I am not talking about secular humanism in writing this presentation. Secular humanism is controlled by the same ego-centric minds as any other 'ism' on this planet. I am telling you about basically uncharted territory for the advancement of human consciousness. Those who have done the work to move into this system of awareness have been very few considering the long history of humans on this planet. It *is* hard work. It is not for the faint of heart or for those without the courage to deal with and accept the fact that they will be different than the vast majority of humans that surround them. The ego part of us all shudders at the idea that we will be different, that there will most likely not be anyone to support us if we do make such a change in cognitive awareness. Unfortunately, this is the price one has to pay at this time, until enough people can work their way through this process of cognitive metamorphosis and come out on the other side to start to make a difference. You have to ask yourself if you have that kind of courage and deep commitment to change yourself or not.

Nietzsche put it this way through the words of Zarathustra:

> *"I want to teach men the sense of their existence, which is the Superman, the lightning out of the dark cloud—man.*
> *But still am I far from them, and my sense speaketh not unto their sense. To men I am still something between a fool and a corpse."*

In bringing this messags to you, I am equal to Nietzsche's Zarathustra, for the sense (cognitive awareness) I am writing about is not the same as your current sense. It is not unlike Jesus' Parable of the Sower found at Mark 4:8-9 about the seeds of conscious advancement being sown and how it can only advance if they hit fertile soil:

> *"Other seeds fell into the good soil, and as they grew up and increased, they yielded a crop and produced thirty, sixty, and a hundredfold."*
> *And He was saying, "He who has ears to hear, let him hear."*

The question you must ask yourself is whether you have the ears to hear the messages of Zarathustra and Jesus. Christianity has completely misconstrued the teachings of Jesus for they were interpretations made by men who had no understanding of the second system of cognition. When Jesus taught of the 'second death', or being 'born again', he was referring to the fact, through the form of parables, that the ego must die in order for the spirit self to come forth. Are you part of that 'good soil' the Sower sought that Jesus referred to so that man's cognitive awareness can multiply and produce a good yield? Do you have the ears to hear the message as it was meant and not as it was misinterpreted by men with no understanding?

The messengers have been few, but the message, no matter how it is phrased or allegorized has always been the same. The messages have all been invitations for others to follow the same path of the messengers. The message to 'follow me' is not one of dependence and exalting the messenger or proclaiming them as deities, but is an invitation for you to do as they did so you can succeed in the same venture into advanced cognitive awareness. Buddhists to this day are following in the footsteps of Buddha, but we have to ask, how many of them are walking in their *own footsteps* to achieve what he did?

All of these teachers stand out as unique, for they all hewed their own paths despite the desires and beliefs of the rest of the herd of humanity. It is easy to misinterpret what another says, to step onto an already cleared path than it is to cut your own path. To walk a well trodden path is the choice of laziness. There is no work, there is no effort required to do that. But to cut your own path requires work. It requires determination, especially if you don't know exactly where the path you are carving out is leading. You will never know where such a path leads if you take the easy road. You will only be coloring inside someone else's predetermined lines, taking their road instead of your own. Nietzsche's Zarathustra echoes these words when he says:

> "A light hath dawned upon me: I need companions—living ones; not dead companions and corpses, which I carry with me where I will.
>
> But I need living companions, *who will follow me because they want to follow themselves*—and to the place where I will."

[Italics mine]

To step into the second cognition one can't be a follower of anyone as their leader. They have to be a leader unto themselves. They have to become totally independent in their quest for cognitive betterment. This is what all the great teachers have taught, yet this singular message has been missed time and time again. Each of these guides or teachers tried, in their own manner, to sow the seeds of awareness, to explain the second form of cognitive awareness, and every time the message was lost through the interpretive cognitive system of the ego, i.e. the seeds have not found fertile soil in which to thrive and grow. The ego demands an authority figure, so all these teachers were either deified or vilified by the people of their time because the cognitive level of the ego only hears what it wants to hear. It is the ego's system of cognitive comprehension that is the perpetrator of misunderstanding throughout all the ages of mankind where spiritual teachings of advanced awareness or enlightenment are concerned. Small minds trying to entrap and interpret larger principles into an acceptable form for their limited box of cognitive perception are the culprits for our misunderstanding such teachings throughout the ages. For this reason, humanity has utterly failed to hear the message as it was meant to be heard. For this reason, humanity finds itself in a state of cognitive arrested development.

Zarathustra's observation about dead companions is a direct reference to those humans still operating under the ego system of mental enslavement, for their consciousness is dead in comparison to living with the second cognition. Don Juan said that such people are 'logs, they are not trees, but dead logs." Jesus instructed his followers to "let the dead bury the dead". What is it that these teachers from different eras and different parts of the world saw that the rest of humanity refuses to see? All of them are referring to human consciousness and what they tried to teach in the alternative that all of them referred to as 'spirit'.

The path of ego consciousness is a dead letter box. The best it can do is devise things outside of itself to change its world. It can invent technologies that seek to create artificial intelligence (AI), yet the ego consciousness refuses to rebuild itself into something more, except in rare cases. The ego consciousness fears the results of AI for the simple reason that it will either take on the properties of its designers (ego) to negative effect, or fear that it will surpass their own limited system of cognitive awareness. Yet the ego consciousness in all of its full blown arrogance proceeds with developing AI rather than seeking how to advance itself. One has to question the rationale behind such thinking, if there is one.

4

Impeccability, Morals and Laws

To fully proceed into the level of the second cognition, one must walk a path of impeccability. Nietzsche used the term virtue, others use the word integrity. To walk with impeccability means to advance into awareness of the fact that you can't trespass on others. You can't violate either their minds or their personal space, for any such violation amounts to a form of tyranny. When a person becomes one with impeccability, unimaginable horizons of perception open up for them. Yet, without personal spiritual integrity, personal impeccability, these horizons will only be unreachable dreams or desires.

Morals are dictated by ego-controlled men to control other ego-controlled men. The ego has no integrity, either personal or otherwise. Your own ego lies to you continually. It is the ultimate con artist. Being the unreliable consciousness that governs the vast majority of humanity, it requires morals and laws to try and prevent it from running rampant. Morals are implemented in order to harness the ego personality, for it has no control over its own self-indulgent selfish desires. Laws are enacted for the very same reason, because the ego possesses no control absent the threat of punishment, and fear is what controls the ego more than any inherent sense of morality.

To be impeccable in spirit and reach the second level of cognitive awareness, one surpasses the needs of any moral dictates or laws used to threaten and control the rampant ego. The impeccable individual inherently knows to not do the wrongs perpetrated by the ego personality without requiring any threat of punishment or damnation as an inhibitor. Morals and laws are unfortunate but necessary mandated controls over egos who lack the impeccability to know or act like civilized beings without the threat of punishment through fear if they don't act according to cultural dictates.

The pursuit of spirit into the second cognition is the path of impeccability. Many Christians detested Nietzsche for his stark criticism of Christianity, but these critics all operated from the sense of their own egos, without an ounce of cognitive understanding about what Nietzsche was doing by exposing the inherent weaknesses in all religions. The ego mentality of his time insured that Nietzsche, who had been a professor, was ostracized and no longer allowed gainful employment after writing *Thus Spake Zarathustra.* The fact that his peers blackballed him and prevented him for pursuing his livelihood only shows the vengeful nature of

53

the narrow ego consciousness. They crucified Christ for similar reasons.

Nietzsche wrote *The Will to Power*, and that is also another of his misunderstood works. According to scholarly assessment, this is mainly because his sister, a vociferous German Nationalist, tainted his writings with her own ideas after his death. The will to power has nothing to do with an ego striving for power over other men, yet he pointedly explained the ego's will to power in the treatise. The will to power is about pushing your own cognitive abilities until you can break through to a new level of cognitive awareness and understanding. Humanity has failed itself throughout its history because it neither has the will to power, nor the understanding of what true power is in the sense of cognitive awareness. In his treatise called *The Antichrist* (§ 6), Nietzsche wrote:

> "Life itself is...the instinct for growth, ... for power:
> where the will to power is lacking there is decline. It
> is my contention that all the supreme values of
> mankind lack this will".

The only drive for power that humanity generally exhibits at this time is for the power that gratifies the selfish needs of the ego. The ego seeks no betterment of itself for it is complete as it is. It only presumes to advance itself through the practice of self-indulgence, self-pity and self-centered selfishness. The ego seeks only to inflate itself in the eyes of others, to stand as a man over men, to be the best, to be the richest, to be the most holy, to be the prettiest, to be the most popular or to be the greatest victim. This is the only form of power the ego understands and it also exemplifies what Nietzsche derisively called "the supreme values of mankind". Under the spell of the ego, there is no will to power of any kind except through the limited perceptual values of the ego and the first cognition. The ego is fully content to be itself, or to be more of itself, but it has no interest in anything that will make it relinquish that position in your mind.

The ego part of each of us is a shallow, self-conscious, fearful program that deals with superficialities. It judges by appearance as much as it makes you worry about your own appearance to others. It makes us want to measure up to standards imposed by forces outside ourselves - our parents, our peers, our religions and our cultures. When you can start to understand your own ego, then it is not that far a leap to perceive our cultures as nothing more than a form of group-ego forcing compliance through its morals and laws.

Morals change according to the whims of other egos mandating what is right and what is not at different times throughout history. This is especially true in religions, where a good majority of the followers of religion are generally just giving their beliefs the necessary lip service to claim acceptance by their god and to be part of a group of like-minded egos. They profess a false morality that most of them do not live, and in that regard, their own ego makes them hypocrites to their alleged beliefs. Their fear of damnation is what keeps them paying tithes and insures the attendance of the most devout. For the ego, the path to heaven is held in place by the threat of Hell.

Laws are not much different than morals. Laws originate when a majority segment of governments, legislatures, or high court judges decide what laws they will impose on whichever faction is on the outs at any given time. These laws are enforced through the threat of fines or punishments. The laws themselves are not respected, they are feared. Once again, the cultural ego forces its will on individual egos. Every nation, religion and individual is hopelessly self-interested. They all want what they want and to hell with any who disagree. Nietzsche put it this way in §768 of *The Will to Power:*

> *"The "ego" subdues and kills: it operates like an organic cell: it is a robber and it is violent. It wants to regenerate itself--pregnancy. It wants to give birth to its god and see all mankind at his feet."*

By quoting Nietzsche, I am not parroting his writings because I am a follower of his philosophies. I am sharing what he said because, to one operating in the second level of cognition, his words are simply obvious truth. Until one has removed their consciousness from the tyranny of their own ego, they cannot remotely comprehend the validity of what the man wrote. The same could be said about the few teachings of Jesus that were not corrupted or omitted by ego-driven religion-makers. Since the beginning of organized Christianity its followers have held their heads bowed and their eyes to the heavens waiting to join their God in his kingdom. Yet Jesus himself told his followers that "the kingdom of heaven lies within." The path to advanced cognitive awareness is the path inward, in fighting and defeating your own ego. Only when this is done will you ever know what Jesus described as "the peace that surpasses all comprehension".

The ego part of all of us is the busy aspect of our mind that requires something to do or it becomes bored. The ego will even play songs in your head to keep itself from being bored. It talks to us in our heads, running a continual stream of chatter, playing games of 'what if' with itself, then manufacturing 'what ifs' on top of 'what ifs'. The ego part of you is constantly second guessing itself, sowing internal doubt and insecurity about how others will perceive it (you). This constant train of chatter is what Don Juan called the *internal dialogue*. Don Juan taught that in order to move into understanding spirit, one has to transcend the ego and turn off the inner dialogue. This is a monumental task of self-discipline. The primary purpose of meditative practices is to discipline one's mind in discovering how to shut off the inner dialogue. In time, both the ego and its inner dialogue will plague you no more and your mind will finally know that 'peace that surpasses all comprehension', what Buddhists refer to as silencing the mind. In your current state of being ruled by your ego, you lack the comprehension of a completely silent and empty mind because it is constantly filled with the ego chattering away day and night. If you doubt this, just try to stop the train of constant thinking you live with and see just how hard it is to make your ego shut up for a mere two minutes.

It is the ego part of us that has convinced us it is ourselves, when in fact it is an impostor, an overlay, a thief of our mind. The real you, the spirit aspect of yourself, lies buried beneath multiple layers of programmed ego illusions and beliefs. In order to reach the second cognition, you are going to have to face and ultimately destroy the mind-hacking program called the ego. This will be the hardest endeavor you will ever undertake and the reward for success cannot be adequately defined because your current level of cognitive awareness has nothing with which to compare it.

Shakespeare once wrote, "To thine own self be true." These are wise words when read in the context of your spirit self, buried beneath the illusions of the ego. To succeed into the second form of cognitive awareness, one first has to know that such a thing exists. One also has to know that there is a part of them that is more expansive in its cognitive abilities than what you can currently perceive. But this hidden part, what Jesus called that 'still silent voice within', cannot be heard over the constant din of the ego. It is only when you remove the ego overlord from the throne of your mind that you will be able to find your true self, your spirit self. Then and only then will that still silent voice be heard to guide you.

For over two thousand years of our known history men and women have been searching for some enigmatic something that they know deep in their gut should exist but has failed to manifest except to a relatively few individuals, and the teachings of those few individuals have, for the most part, been turned into the foundations of world religions or mystical esoteric traditions. Many genuine seekers have an internal drive to know what this enigmatic something is, but they are all seeking the proverbial needle in the haystack. The needle you have been seeking is the second cognition. Unless you have read the Don Juan teachings by Carlos Castenada, you will not find this needle in any teaching stated as cogently and directly as did Don Juan. And even then, the needle of this teaching amounted to maybe a short paragraph or two out of ten books written by Carlos Castenada. Castenada himself never saw the importance of this revelation of truth. Castenada *never* comprehended the teachings.

The pop New Age culture is rife with modern forms of the Western guru, who themselves are not that much different than the Eastern gurus. Many of them bask in the limelight of their fame as presumed masters of consciousness, but the question must be asked that if these people are as enlightened as they claim to be, why hasn't a single one of them told you the simple truth about the second cognition? If their consciousness is as remotely advanced as they themselves claim, then why have none of them related this simple yet powerful truth?

Neither Jesus nor Buddha wrote anything during their lifetimes. Their teachings were all oral teachings, primarily due to the fact that most of the people of their times were stone illiterate. We have two of the major world religions formed by second-hand interpretations of people who lacked the understanding of what their teachers taught. This form of second-hand interpretation is what has led to sectarianism in all religions, and it is also the same type of second-hand interpretations that make up the New Age movement with its attempted homogenization of global supernatural and mystical belief systems.

I ask the reader to remember if they ever played the 'Whisper Game' sometime in their lives. If you have not played this game, it is easy to do. Gather 8-10 people or more in a circle and have one person whisper something to the person sitting next to them. By the time the whispered message returns to the original sender, the message is totally corrupted and nothing like what the originator said to begin with. All of our religious teachings are subject to same premise found in the Whisper Game. No two people interpret a message the same way, particularly parables. If there is any chance of alternate interpretation, someone will make it, and this is exactly what has happened in all religious teachings as well as our presumed historical accountings. All we have gotten is watered-down, misunderstood interpretations of religion and mystical traditions, for they are all predicated on the interpretive systems of the individual interpreters. Virtually all the information we get is second-hand information, and where matters of spirit are concerned, the messengers have all been subject to the limited cognitive system of the ego, who continually misinterpret the true meaning about the second cognition. Given this scenario, it is little wonder than mankind has not advanced its system of cognition for tens of thousands of years.

As a species we all hang our hats at the door of our authority figures, yet all of these presumed authority figures are just as prone to misinterpretations as you are. We are especially gullible when it comes to trusting so-called authorities on matters of spirit. We assume that because they speak to us in riddles that they are somehow more enlightened than we are, that if we can figure out the riddles in which they speak, that we will find enlightenment. I will give you another perspective to consider. For those who are seeking understanding on the spirit path, have you ever thought that the reason all these gurus speak in riddles is because they don't have a clue themselves, that they are running a scam simply because so many others buy the malarkey? Have you ever considered that they have only adopted the ages old line about the supernatural and have simply repackaged it for a new gullible audience? Have you ever considered that they speak in riddles because what they are selling is simply supernatural nonsense that has been wooing the masses of humanity for untold generations? It seems to be a riddle because it is *not meant* to be figured out. It is a supernatural road to nowhere, yet it has become a multi-billion dollar industry. Sharp egos have figured out that the supernatural sells, generation after generation, and people are *still* buying into the nonsense.

In all fairness, I have to say that there are millions of genuine seekers around the planet, all fumbling in the haystack of supernatural hogwash trying to find the needle that may explain things for them. Most have never even considered the possibility of a second form of cognitive awareness than the one they currently operate under. As with many things, one needs a key to understand something in order to open a door that seems to be locked and impenetrable. You are now armed with a key that opens a door to a second form of cognitive awareness. Many of you have been searching for understanding, groping at supernatural strands of swill in order to make sense out of what your gut instinct tells you should be there, yet none of the modern gurus have explained this simple premise. I have not had to resort to mystical riddle-posing in order to explain this. I have not had to *initiate* you into this knowledge as so many so-called mystery schools claim that you need to be in order to understand the quest for higher level awareness. I have simply told you what you are looking for without all the supernatural or mystical twaddle that people throughout the ages feel is necessary for understanding matters of spirit. Now that you know what it is that you are seeking, that this second system of cognition is attainable without all the mystical hogwash, you have to know how to achieve this breakthrough in consciousness. Knowing about it removes the first hurdle of understanding. Getting there is harder than just knowing it is there.

5

The Factor of Cognitive Dissonance

What is known as the *Theory of Cognitive Dissonance* was first proposed by Leon Festinger in 1957. According to Festinger's theory, what he termed cognitive dissonance occurs when someone encounters an idea or concept that challenges a belief held by that individual, which causes psychological uncomfortability. The second premise of the theory notes that when one encounters such psychological dissonance, that they will do everything they can to restore what he called 'consonance', including avoiding any situation or information that may present the individual with such psychological discomfort or increase their sense of cognitive dissonance.

What this means in layman's terms is that if one is confronted with an idea or situation that psychologically 'rocks their world', it generates a fear response inside of us, leading either to denial or acceptance of the new information or situation. The third alternative to cognitive dissonance is a form of irrational reasoning perpetrated to keep the belief in place despite proof or claims to the contrary. In other terms, this can be called apologetics, and the enforcers of religions have used apologetics for centuries to defend their beliefs in the face of challenges to the contrary. People turn to apologetics as a form of defending a position they are neither willing to deny nor alter.

The simplest example of a situation of cognitive dissonance I can give that I think anyone can understand is to ask you to imagine that you were brought up in a household with loving parents and siblings, and that your whole perception is that they are your family. Then one day it is revealed to you that they are not your natural parents, but that you were adopted as a baby. I ask you to imagine the inner turmoil that such a revelation would have on your perceptual awareness. Everything you thought and believed about your family and yourself was suddenly thrown out the window. Your whole perception about yourself, your life, your family has proven to be a fabrication. The first response would probably be to ask if the person telling you was joking. When they tell you that they are telling the truth, the next instinct is where you get like an electric jolt of fear all over your body, then denial kicks in as a result of the cognitive dissonance between what you thought was real versus what you have been told (or discovered) is real. This electrical jolt of fear is a natural occurrence of cognitive dissonance when the ego finds its perceptual world shaken to its core.

This may be an extreme example of cognitive dissonance, but I think it is a situation that everyone can relate to if they were to imagine themselves in that position. When Festinger writes about consonance, he is speaking about attaining some form of mental balance in the face of the new information that shatters a deeply held belief structure. Operating under our current system of cognitive awareness we have become comfortable with our perceived definitions of the world and our reality. Whenever we encounter anything that threatens the structure of that perception, cognitive dissonance occurs. The human response to such psychological dissonance is to deny what they have discovered or been told, and try to rebuild their cognitive equilibrium (consonance). Denial is the most representative form of avoiding cognitive dissonance.

As one moves toward the second form of cognitive awareness, they will be confronted many times with bouts of cognitive dissonance as they discover that their perceptions about the world under their current cognitive system are proven to be false. When one experiences one of these bouts of cognitive dissonance, a jolt of fear hits the body as the realization sets in that what they formerly believed to be a truth is shown to be a lie. One gets a sinking feeling in their stomach when such a truth reveals a former belief to be a lie. The more deeply held the belief is, the stronger the fear reaction is when such a realization sets in. The wisest course for a person to take when they encounter these bouts of cognitive dissonance is to accept what is shown to be true rather than denying it. Most people, due to the fear response of having one of their belief systems shattered, choose to deny or ignore the alternative truth and work to establish some sense of normalcy (consonance) back into the old system of cognition. If you fall prey to this fear response and give in to it, your ego will have won the battle and you will not progress further on your quest into the second cognition.

Fear is the tool of the ego. The ego part of you uses fear against you to maintain its control over your mind and keep its perceptual kingdom in place. If you cave in to fear you will never advance into the second cognition. Fear is a very powerful deterrent and the ego knows exactly how to play the fear mechanism in all of us. What the ego can't force us to deny or ignore, the ego will steer us away from through fear. As Don Juan taught, fear is the first enemy of one trying to advance into spiritual awareness. If you can overcome the fear whenever you have your perceptions eroded, then you are strong enough to proceed on the path to advanced cognitive awareness. If you can't transcend your own personal fears, give up the necessary illusions of your ego's perceptual belief system in favor of greater truths, then you will never succeed.

These perceptual beliefs are not all centered around religions or supernatural beliefs. Each nation and culture has its own form of historical mythology. Many of the perceptual illusions you will have to shed are historical illusions about your perceived reality. To move into the second system of cognition, you will be required to study things that you disagree with in order to see an alternative interpretation of what you think is truth. It is the easy road to avoid what we disagree with and only read what feeds our current perceptual ego requirements. The easy road is the road of complacency. It will not lead one to the second cognition. Continuing to digest only information that feeds and supports your current belief systems will not advance your consciousness, as that only amounts to building your current perceptual walls higher.

Because the path to higher-level awareness is fraught with these fears, the vast majority of people lack what Nietzsche called 'the will to power'. One has to have the desire to succeed at any cost or their efforts are doomed from the start. One has to be willing to have their perceptual world turned on its head in order to progress into a new system of perceptual awareness. If you don't feel that you have that type of internal determination or drive, then you may as well keep chasing mystical rainbows, for the second cognition will be ever out of your reach.

The present system of human cognition is about the easy road. Oh, we may have rebels and malcontents, but each and every one of them is still driven by limited ego desires. To reach the second cognition requires stamina, dedication and discipline. If you have none of these qualities inside you, then you will never reach what you are seeking. You are safer embracing myths of the mystical and supernatural, (or in the case of science and rationalism, denying them), for you do not have the necessary requirements to gain that awareness. The path to willful evolution requires the will to power. This is not the same as what we know as will power. The will to power is an internal drive to attain something that you know exists on a deep level inside yourself. The will to power is not wishing or hoping something is true, as most belief systems unfortunately are.

Since this will to power is an internal knowing from some source you have not yet been able to tap into, it also means that the answers to discovering this also lie within yourself and your mind.

Advancement is going to entail challenging virtually everything you believe about your perceptual reality. This choice for willful evolution will cost you. You will no longer be like the people around you. You will feel discomfort as you progress into the second cognition when you realize that you will no longer have a point of cognitive relationship with people operating in the first cognition. You can see and understand where they are, cognitively speaking, but they can't remotely comprehend your level of perceptual comprehension. You have to be strong in yourself to be able to function in their world while your cognitive awareness advances into realms you can't currently comprehend.

This separation of cognitive systems is very difficult to deal with in its early stages, for none of us wants to break away from the herd, but you can't advance yourself and hang on to what you are trying to transcend at the same time. So before embarking on this plan of your own willful evolution, you have to consider the cost and whether you are willing to pay it. If you do not have the supreme will to power, to be different while the herd is marching in lockstep, then don't embark on this journey. I apprise you of these challenges, not to dissuade you from your efforts, but more to inform you of what you will encounter along the way.

For all the teachers who have reached the next level of cognitive awareness they find themselves in a situation similar to this analogy. Imagine that two people are taken to an art exhibition to view a painting. One of the people is blindfolded before the painting is presented to them. Now, the blindfolded person is asked to describe the painting. The blindfolded person has no sense (sight) to see the painting nor describe it, but they are told the painting is right in front of them. When the blindfolded person fails to describe the picture in the painting, the one who is not blindfolded is asked to describe the picture to the blindfolded person. As the person with sight works to describe the picture, the blindfolded individual starts to manufacture mental images of the picture as it is described in their mind's eye. As the picture is described, the blindfolded person builds an internal imaginary image of what they are being told the picture looks like.

When the sighted person is done explaining the picture, the blindfolded person has created a perceptual image of what the picture is presumed to look like based on the description provided by the person with sight. When the blindfold is removed and the person can finally see the picture, what they see is nothing like what they imagined.

The role of any teacher into the second state of cognitive awareness is that of the person describing the painting. No matter how they explain it, the imaginary interpretive senses of the one blindfolded always come up with something totally different than what was related. When trying to explain the second cognition, the perceptual range of people operating in the primary cognitive state most humans do, attributes the explanations about the second cognition to something mystical, magical or supernatural, for the simple reason that they have no framework within the first cognition to comprehend what is being described. In essence, they are blindfolded and can't see the picture.

Throughout the ages, it has been the limited imagination of those wearing the blindfold who have taken it upon themselves to describe the painting, and in every case, the image is always incorrect. It leads to erroneous suppositions and we find ourselves today where matters of spirit all amount to a case of the blind leading the blind. This is the main reason that the majority of people can't grasp principles of spirit, because those wearing the blindfold, those who have never actually experienced the second cognition, have made themselves the authorities predicated upon their own lack of understanding and incorrect suppositions about what it actually is. Because they can't comprehend it themselves, they paint pictures of something mystical or supernatural, for that is all their minds can create as an explanation.

Virtually all spiritual teachings these days, and throughout the ages, are predicated on the misinterpretations and misrepresentations of the blindfolded individuals telling you what they claim they see, when in fact they see nothing. As Jesus related in Luke 6:39-40:

> *"Can a blind man lead a blind man? Will they not both fall into a pit? A student is not above his teacher, but everyone who is fully trained will be like his teacher."*

This blindness is what served as the foundation for the formation of all the so-called esoteric doctrines, mystery schools and religions. It has been a mystery over the ages, and remains a mystery, because those trying to interpret the teachings are merely *speculating* about what they *think* it means, not comprehending what it actually is. Since they have no firsthand knowledge of what they are claiming to know as teachers and gurus, they rely on the speculators about consciousness from previous ages to support their misinterpretations. In this manner does the primary cognition of humanity still wander around in the maze of spiritual supernaturalism and basic mystical superstition. It truly is a system of the cognitively blind leading the cognitively blind. The philosophers of today follow blindly in the footsteps of their cognitively blind predecessors, all arguing in their own fashion how to reinterpret the misinterpreted words of wisdom of the presumed ancient philosophies, and all of them intellectual defenders of the first system of cognition.

Thus Spake Zarathustra was Friedrich Nietzsche's first 'philosophical' work. This suggests that everything he wrote after this proclamation of his own heightened awareness, through the voice of Zarathustra, was a continuing criticism of the limitations of human consciousness operating under the primary system of cognition. The defenders of the first cognition vilified Nietzsche for his writings during his lifetime and those that didn't vilify him simply called his presentations 'existential philosophy', for that is the only way their limited consciousness could perceive what he wrote in their operating from the first cognition. They lacked the mental and cognitive capability to remotely understand what he was trying to teach as truth of spirit and advanced cognitive abilities.

Modern psychology came into being out of the school of philosophy. The field of psychology is considered 'soft science' because it cannot pass the scrutiny of an empirical scientific study. All of the work of psychologists is theoretical in nature because it cannot pass empirical scrutiny. This is why Festinger's *Theory of Cognitive Dissonance* is a *theory*. His theory has been studied and tested enough that it is considered a valid theory in the field of Psychology. From the standpoint of one who has stepped into the second level of cognitive awareness, cognitive dissonance is not theoretical, it is an actuality of experience.

Plato, also considered to be one of the most brilliant ancient Greek philosophers, hinted at the concept of cognitive dissonance in Socrates' *Allegory of the Cave*. Although he didn't use that specific term, the circumstances he 'philosophized' about in the *Allegory of the Cave* makes similar observations. Since Plato was able to make that speculative rendering of cognitive dissonance in the *Allegory*, it proves unequivocally that the same mindset was present in ancient human cognition as much as it is prevalent in our system of modern cognitive awareness to this day.

Plato studied under Socrates, another great teacher who left absolutely nothing written behind to attest to his knowledge or understanding on issues of cognition. We are left with the second-hand writings of Plato to relate how he interpreted what Socrates taught him. At this late stage we can only wonder what Socrates knew that Plato didn't understand and subsequently related in his own philosophical treatises. Scholars have debated the meaning of Plato's rendering about the trial of Socrates found in *The Last Days of Socrates*; whether it is remotely accurate in its telling. Segment 2 of the treatise, *Apology*, shows us another man (Socrates) who had stepped into the second cognition and was tried and handed the death penalty because he just plain made all the intellectual and religious authorities of his time mad at him for his exposing their cognitive insufficiencies in regard to wisdom. The trumped up charge of religious defiance of the gods was the weapon used to convict him. Are you starting to see a repeating reactionary pattern to those who reach the second cognition at the hands of the defenders of the first cognition yet?

Nietzsche used the same word, 'herd', as did Socrates in his time. Jesus more politely referred to the herd as a catch of small fishes in his allegories. Yet in virtually every case, the herd mentality never listens and always responds the same. Socrates was prosecuted for challenging the religious standards of the Greeks through trying to explain the second cognition and was dealt the death penalty by the herd mentality of his time. Jesus was crucified for challenging the cognitive and religious mores of his day. Lao Tzu, the composer of the Tao Te Ching, walked off the world stage around 2600 BCE in dismay and disgust at the insanity of the herd mentality that surrounded him. Nietzsche was deprived of pursuing his livelihood by the Christianity-supporting peers of his day because the herd mentality of his time refused to listen to what he tried to teach them about the overman and the second cognition. It seems that only Buddha and Don Juan may have escaped such circumstances, but if so, they are rare exceptions to the rule. I have little doubt that the message contained within these pages will be met with equal scorn from all corners by protectors of the herd mentality of the egoistic first cognition.

73

<u>6</u>

<u>*Jesus and the Second System of Cognition*</u>

The pop New Age movement is filled with a mixture of doctrines, all seeking to become homogenized into a sort of non-religious religion. It claims to not be about religion, but instead represents 'spiritual' development. Most of the modern New Age movement was spawned and sponsored in recent history by the Russian medium Madame Helena Blavatsky and her disciple Alice Bailey through the advent of the quasi-religion called Theosophy. Blavatsky and Bailey laid the foundation for the modern New Age movement through their own particular brand of mystic revelations - in Blavatsky's case, via messages from a purported etheric Ascended Tibetan Master she called Koot Hoomi. Blavatsky reported to have received much of her spiritual information through psychic channeling from good old Koot.

It was out of the craze of mediums, starting in about the 1840's, that Blavatsky made her platform into establishing her own brand of religion - Theosophy - by creating the Theosophical Society in 1875. I am not going into her history as I leave it up to those interested to do their own research into the subject as I did. That is one of the tasks of moving into the second cognition - do your own work!

Alice Bailey got involved with the Theosophical Society in 1917. Although her own writings did not exactly mirror those of Blavatsky, she allegedly received her information about the *Ageless Wisdom Teachings* from her own *etheric* 'Tibetan' Ascended Master Djwal Khul. Bailey developed the concept of an Age of Aquarius and a unified global 'spirit of religion'. Bailey and her husband, Foster, created a publishing company in 1922 known as Lucifer Publishing, Co. The next year they changed the name to Lucis Publishing Co., today also known as Lucis Trust.

Alice Bailey's Lucis Trust was an organization that became the "spiritual foundation of the United Nations". Until recently Lucis Trust had offices at the U.N. Headquarters. I relate this much information to show you that most of the modern pop New Age movement has a political agenda behind its teachings, despite the profound ignorance of the origins of New Age philosophies and ideas embraced by most of its followers. Again, this information is readily available for those who want to understand the origin and nature of their presumed spiritual beliefs, so if you want to know more, do your own research.

From the purported medium craze of the 1840's and Blavatsky and Bailey's forays into psychically channeling alleged Tibetan Masters in later decades, we move into the current New Age craze for people claiming to channel all sorts of entities. It takes little effort to find purportedly channeled messages by Jesus, Mary Magdalene, the Archangels, space aliens and an untold cast of hundreds of channeled entities in books and on the internet. Many people are hooked on reading these mystical and supernatural channelings and are anxiously waiting for each and every new message by the 'heavenly host' of channeled entities. Who these entities are or may be goes beyond the scope of this book, so I will leave it here to address more realistic issues in regard to understanding what people refer to as spirit teachings.

Part of the conglomerate doctrines of the New Age is the inclusion of the concepts of Gnosticism, a sect of mostly philosophers cum religionists who operated in a parallel time frame of the establishment of the early Roman form of Christianity. In time, they were deemed heretics by the Roman Church and either hunted down and killed, converted, or went undergound with their teachings. The word *gnosis* comes from the ancient Greek and translates to mean' knowledge', or 'knowing'. For hundreds of years the only information that was available about the Gnostics and what they wrote was to be found in polemics written by Roman Catholic authors condemning their heresy. In 1945, two years before the Dead Sea Scrolls were unearthed, what has become known as the Nag Hammadi Library was discovered in a cave in Nag Hammadi, Egypt. The scrolls, packaged in urns like the Dead Sea Scrolls, are the most comprehensive source of Gnostic writings ever to be unearthed.

Today, you will find no shortage of New Age acolytes professing, in their profound ignorance, what the Gnostics allegedly said that supports their belief system. Most of these people have never read all of the writings found in the Nag Hammadi Library, so they make the false assumption that there was some sort of doctrinal agreement from the ancient Gnostics. Yet it only takes a reading of the Nag Hammadi material to discover that there was no homogenized thought in the writings considered Gnostic. Much of the Gnostic writing is purely philosophical. A good quantity of the writings are about Jesus, but according to whichever philosophy each Gnostic writer embraced, the character of Jesus and what he said changes as much as a chameleon changes color. Within all the Gnostic literature found in the desert in 1945, there is one document that I think most accurately relates some of what the man known as Jesus taught.

I know there are two sides to the argument about Jesus. There is no historical evidence that can be presented that proves he ever lived, and that is the argument that Atheists and disbelievers cite as the foundation for their arguments that he never existed. On the other side we have the staunch believers that he was the Son of God and their personal Savior. In the middle we have people that acknowledge his potential existence, but consider him only a man and a wise teacher. From the standpoint of my own experience, I have to fall on the middle ground in that regard, and this is based on my own personal experience and the understanding I am trying to relate to you in this book.

What I find the most relevant of all the Gnostic texts in regard to the sayings of Jesus is *The Gospel of Thomas,* because in many places it accurately portrays the sayings of someone who has evolved into the second level of cognitive awareness trying to explain it to those who lacked understanding. I will provide a few examples of those sayings from *The Gospel of Thomas* with my own explanations in order to help you see what was written almost 2,000 years ago and how it directly relates to what I am trying to show you now.

> Jesus said, "*Let him who seeks continue seeking until [he] finds; and when he finds, he will become troubled. When he becomes troubled, he will be amazed, and he will rule over the All.*"

What Jesus is relating about becoming troubled once one finds what they are seeking, it is an allegorical reference to the cognitive dissonance written about previously. No one moves into the second cognition without experiencing the pain of cognitive dissonance. No one moves into the second cognition unless they are seeking conscious understanding and keep seeking it until they find it as I did.

> Jesus said, "*If those who lead you say unto you: Behold, the Kingdom is in heaven, then the birds of the heaven will be before you. If they say unto you: It is in the sea, then the fish will be before you. But the Kingdom is within you, and it is outside of you. When you know yourselves, then shall you be known, and you shall know that you are the sons of the living Father. But if ye do not know yourselves, then you are in poverty, and you are poverty.*"

Here again, Jesus is echoing what I have shared in this volume so far. Until you know yourself, until you set aside the ego and realize the true nature of who you are, your spirit self will not be known to you, and you will dwell in the poverty of the first cognition and you will be your own source of poverty for continuing to embrace that level of cognitive awareness, rather than evolving yourself into a state of higher-level awareness. This is not just my interpretation of the passage. In light of everything I have shared with you, reread the passage and see if you can come up with a better explanation for what he is saying in the foregoing passage.

> Jesus said, *"Know what is before thy face, and what [is]hidden from thee shall be revealed unto thee; for there is nothing hidden which shall not be made manifest."*

In this passage Jesus is telling us that the truths that create that cognitive dissonance within ourselves lie in front of our eyes. These truths are all around you, yet the vast majority of us choose to deny or avoid them rather than find them and accept them. For the most part, we refuse to even look for these truths. We each have to recognize these uncomfortable truths in order to have that which is hidden from our current level of cognition manifest into our perceptual reality. Look at what is in front of you. Quit denying things because they contradict what you believe. When you acknowledge the truths you want to avoid, only then will what is hidden (or denied) be revealed to you.

> And he said, *"Man is like a wise fisherman, who cast his net into the sea and drew it up from the sea full of small fish. Among them the wise fisherman found a large good fish. He threw down all the small fish into the sea; he chose the large fish without trouble. He that hath ears to hear, let him hear."*

In this passage Jesus is talking about finding 'worthy' students willing to understand spirit. The small fish are representational of humanity operating under the ego system of cognition, the herd. The large fish is representational of the few who have the determination to succeed in their personal quest into the second cognition against all odds. The guide or teacher will not waste their time on the small fish because he is wise enough to know that the small fish will not let go of their cognitive system in order to evolve themselves. The question we must all ask ourselves is whether we are one of the small fish, or are we the large fish? Whoever has ears to hear, let them listen to this message.

> Jesus said, "*When you see him who was not born of woman, throw yourselves down on your face and worship him. He is your father.*"

This passage is probably one of the most confusing statements from Jesus in *The Gospel of Thomas* for a couple of reasons. In the first instance, we ask ourselves what is a person who is not born of woman? This question can only be appropriately answered when one understands cognitive willful evolution. When one moves from the primary human cognitive system into the second cognition through their own will to power, they become 'self-created' individuals. In essence, they make themselves a new person and are therefore 'not born of woman'. When Jesus uses the word worship, it is not in the context that we understand worship in a religions sense. One of the definitions of worship in Webster's dictionary is "*reverence offered a divine being or supernatural power; **also :** an*

80

act of expressing such reverence." Let's remove the words divine and supernatural power and we have a definition of worship that means to respect the one not born of woman. By stating that such a person is your father, Jesus means that the person not born of woman is the one who can guide you to also be a person not born of woman. You may or may not wish to accept this interpretation, but that is what it means. As to physical prostration, no one who has transcended into the second cognition would ever expect anyone to prostrate themselves on their behalf. Such a demand or expectation would prove that they are not what they claim to be and are still operating from the standpoint of ego glorification. The chances are that that part of the passage was inserted by religious interpreters rather than what he actually said.

> Jesus said, "*I will give you that which eye has not seen, an ear has not heard, and hand has not touched, and which has not entered into the heart of man.*"

This passage should be self-explanatory when it comes to describing the second cognition, for the simple reason that to one operating in the first cognition, it has never occurred to them that such a thing as the second cognition even exists. When one reaches the second cognition they will perceive things that no eye has seen and no ear has heard in the first cognition. I know this all sounds tremendously mystical, but I ask you to consider this, what exactly it is you think you are going to attain if you achieve *enlightenment?*

Jesus said, *"I stood in the midst of the world, and I appeared to them in flesh. I found them all drunk, I found none among them thirsting; and my soul was afflicted for the sons of men, for they are blind in their heart and they do not see. For empty came they into the world, seeking also to depart empty from the world. But now they are drunk. When they have thrown off their wine, then will they repent."*

This passage is a testament to anyone who has attained the second cognition. All of humanity is intoxicated with the ego cognition, and as such they all live in the spiritual poverty of not knowing any better. Even worse, they exhibit no thirst to know anything better. We come into this world, are indoctrinated into the primary system of cognition, and then simply accept it as all there is. If we seek any kind of escape from the morass of the ego world, we turn to the supernatural and the idea of mystical messiahs to save us because that is the drug the ego needs to sustain its fantasies about spirit. From one living within the second cognition, it does make one's soul ache to observe such pointless abuse of our lives when one knows there is something better that most of humanity is missing in their intoxication of the first cognition. This is the last saying I will share. If the reader wants more they can dig it out for themselves and find their own understanding of the teachings.

7

Plato's Allegory of the Cave and the Self-created

In Plato's *Allegory of the Cave*, Plato describes a set of prisoners who can't move their heads but can only look straight ahead, and all they can see are shadows cast upon a wall manipulated by people in front of a huge fire that makes the shadows project onto a wall in front of the prisoners. This being all that they know, their whole perception of the world is defined by these shadows. When one of them is finally led out of the cave into the sunlight and then brought back to describe his experience to the other prisoners, they all balk and claim that such a thing cannot be true, for the only reality from which they can gauge their perception is the shadows cast on the wall. In their stark ignorance of anything different, they deny the existence of the real world that exists outside the cave.

We all start out in an equivalent world where everyone's perception is basically the same - the realm of the ego. If someone advances into a greater system of cognition, as the one who ventured into the sunlight and returned, and then tries to tell others of their experiences, they can't remotely perceive what that person is talking about because it goes beyond the limits of their own perceptual awareness. The usual response is denial that such a thing can be possible. As those who stayed in the cave denied the truth of what the one who was taken into the sunlight revealed, the perception of the ego just as easily discounts the idea that someone else can achieve a different level of cognitive awareness because it goes beyond the comprehension level of ego cognition - unless it is supernatural or mystical in nature.

In defense of its own system of self-enforced ignorance, the ego becomes defensive and works to destroy the messenger for the message they present. Just the same as those who viewed the shadows on the wall as the definition of their reality, the consciousness of the ego does exactly the same thing. It defends what is knows in defiance of what could be known. In this regard, the ego becomes an agent for tyranny by maintaining its own strident world view and defends it from all who would challenge that viewpoint. The question every genuine seeker must ultimately ask themselves is whether they want to advance into the unknown or defend the known view of reality that they currently embrace. To be a defender of this perceptual reality is the realm of the ego, to advance beyond it into the sunlight, the defender (ego) has to go by the way side. In the *Allegory*, who was the wiser, the one who had experienced the outside and the sunlight, or the ones who stayed locked in the cave defending their own limited perception?

Many sincere seekers are looking for what they *presume* enlightenment to be. In the last chapter I mentioned the term 'self-created'. This is going to be a complex discussion and I expect few, if any, to understand what I am trying to relate. Some of those who have looked into certain spiritual schools have run across the concept of God being referred to as the 'self-created one'. At first glance, the concept of anyone being self-created defies our system of logic. One can't be self-created if they had parents, etc. But this limited perspective deals only with our limited perception as I related when I explained about the one not born of woman in the last chapter. I am taking things as a given in this presentation. If you don't accept these givens, it is no concern of mine, nor do I need to hear picayune protests from the uninformed in regard to challenging the givens presented here.

To be self-created, one has to attain a singularity of conscious awareness. This doesn't mean you create your form in incarnation (your body), it means you are totally in charge of creating your spiritual self - your own cognitive awareness. From the standpoint of the soul, each incarnation in the reincarnational cycle gives us an opportunity to become self-created, free, consciously aware individuals. The vast majority of the time, we miss that opportunity; our bodies die, the ego disconnects from the soul, and the soul reincarnates once again to try becoming self-created once more, and the cycle repeats ad infinitum, with very few ever becoming self-created.

In the Don Juan teachings, Don Juan expressed the idea of maintaining his individual consciousness even after facing death of his form. To him, (and to me), conscious awareness and freedom in maintaining that integrity of personal consciousness in the face of eternity is all that matters. To reach the point that he did in that regard, is the path of self-creation.

To become self-created means that one transcends any aspect of subservience to any concept that holds our consciousness bound and restrained. It amounts to reaching a state of total autonomy of consciousness, to be answerable to no God or other concept whereby we view ourselves in any manner as lesser beings compared to any other consciousness in creation. It is reaching a state of total freedom of consciousness, but one must also assume total responsibility for what they do in order to do this. One cannot reach that state of being self-created if they lack impeccability.

Being self-created is the knowledge that you are individually and totally responsible for the development of your own consciousness. One will never reach the state of being self-created so long as they continue to follow the ideas and dictates of another. If you are a follower of any doctrine, you are not self-created, you are merely following the ideas or beliefs of others who came before you - in other words, your consciousness is not totally free, it remains bound to the ideas and belief structures of others. Every follower of any doctrine or dogma is only a contributor to perpetuating any given belief system, spiritual or otherwise. They are not creating their own pathway to the second cognition. They are not independent and free consciousnesses, they are slaves to the ideas of others.

Every consciousness in existence has the path to self-creation open to them, but few have figured out, or have even been instructed that such an option exists. It is easy to mouth the belief that 'I am God', and even easier for the ego personality to actually believe such tripe - even that 'we are all God', blah blah. These are merely statements without cognitive understanding of the real meaning of any of it. Even giving lip-service to the idea that we are all God is indicative of a subservient mindset to the principle that some God exists and we are simply some lesser part of that God concept.

To be self-created in one's consciousness means that they are no longer consciously bound by faux rules of morality or concepts of right or wrong beyond what their own consciousness dictates. From the standpoint of an ego, this concept can barely be conceived without casting immature moral aspersions on the idea or creating tyrants. The ego cannot understand spiritual impeccability, so it can not remotely perceive the idea of total cognitive autonomy of being self-created. It is such a foreign concept to that cognitive system that it can only be denied and criticized - not unlike an ant assaulting an elephant.

In all of my studies I have never come across this concept justly discussed by anyone. One may find references to God as being self-created, but that is where the whole idea stops. So I invite the reader to entertain the idea that consciousness evolves. With enough evolution of your consciousness, with enough clarity in understanding, with absolute impeccability of spirit, one can reach that state of being consciously self-created. Your soul has spent lifetimes in incarnation seeking to advance its consciousness, but advance to what? A closer union with some presumed God or Goddess? To achieve some fictional 'oneness' in some sort of collective cosmic hive mind? What do you or your soul think you are advancing towards? The answer is to become self-created.

I have taken great pains to try and reveal to you what the path to enlightenment means and I have covered some of the aspects of what willful evolution to become a self-created consciousness entails. There are many people who have experienced brief moments of enlightenment. Many of these people are still operating primarily in the first system of cognition, so when they have these brief encounters with spiritual revelations, they make the mistaken assumption that they have achieved enlightenment. Many others experience a brief epiphany one time and spend the rest of their lives trying to regain the experience. In comparative allegory, one who has a brief encounter with enlightenment is like someone who gets their feet wet at the ocean's shore and feels qualified to describe the depths of the ocean from that brief experience of getting their feet wet.

The second cognition is a congitive awareness deeper than the ocean, and it takes more than a singular brief encounter to dwell there on a daily basis. Those who get a brief glimpse, who's egos feel they are now experts into that level of cognitive awareness, are not only deceiving themselves, but deceiving the millions who buy their books and attend their seminars. One brief glimpse into the second cognition is not enough to make anyone an expert. It is, however, meant to be an invitation to investigate more deeply and continue to advance your consciousness. The problem is that so few continue advancing and feel they have 'arrived', that they are *enlightened,* and therefore cease their journey.

One does not have to move into the second cognition to have an experience from spirit. In fact, most people have their first experience of brief enlightenment while they are still deeply rooted in the first cognition and their ego is still fully in charge. What brief bit of enlightenment they may have experienced has given them a taste of heightened awareness, but that brief experience is only a match in the dark to advancing more fully into the second system of cognitive awareness. When one falls prey to their ego and thinks they are qualified to tell others what enlightenment is from that brief moment of experienced clarity, they have met what Don Juan called the second enemy of one on the spirit path, and that is clarity.

If one falls prey to their ego, they will not lose that clarity, but they will have ceased seeking knowledge and understanding because they have allowed their egos to use their limited encounter with clarity as a foundation to fortify their own ego's system of cognition. Their ego makes them believe that they now have the answer to the ages old quest for enlightenment and it chooses to become an authority to others rather than continuing more deeply into the second state of cognitive awareness to gain more understanding. Being partially enlightened and trying to teach to another is more dangerous than one who has never had the experience, for neither the student nor the presumed teacher will have a correct assessment of what the second cognition is all about.

It takes years of self-evaluation and challenging the ego at every turn before one can move firmly into the second level of cognitive awareness. A brief experience, which can happen to anyone at any time, is no foundation for understanding that level of awareness on a permanent basis, it is merely an invitation to move further ahead. Through the long and arduous course of destroying your ego and advancing your cognitive awareness more deeply into the second cognition, you will discover that the door that opens into the second cognition is in fact only a beginning, not an ending.

Do not let me leave you with the mistaken impression that if you step into the second form of cognitive awareness that your journey is over, it is only the start. Although you will be able to see the handicaps of the first cognition, you will be stepping into a new world of perceptual awareness. The knowledge of the universe lies before you, but you are a babe in the woods when you step into this new system of cognitive awareness. Your lifetime of experience operating in the first cognition is of little use to you, for in the second cognition the rules are different. To venture out to discover what is 'out there' is going to take a lot of work, and what you discover will shake the foundations of the perceptual world you just left. It is more challenging than moving to a foreign country and trying to not only learn the language of the inhabitants, but to also understand its cultural nuances. Virtually everything you thought you knew will have to be tossed out because the universe and how it functions is different than your wildest imaginings.

You will discover that the universe is filled with consciousness. At first you are going to find this disconcerting for you are going to discover things that destroy the foundations of what you thought reality was. You are going to want to deny what you may discover. If you are not cautious in your venturing out there with other consciousnesses, you may find yourself in sticky situations. You are going to have to proceed with caution and you are going to have to learn judgment through keen discernment.

In the second cognition you are not going to be able to rely solely on what you think, you will have to learn to rely on other forms of sensory input. You will get personal revelations, after which your thinking processes will engage to analyze what these revelations reveal to you. As we currently function in the first cognition, we think before anything. We assume that everything we want to know comes from the thinking process. When you step into the second cognition and develop yourself, you work more from a state of intuitive awareness first, then think about what your intuition is telling you second. It takes a number of years to learn how to function in this manner, so don't sell yourself the idea that just because you have advanced from the first cognition into the second that your work is finished. Just as you have to walk the hard path to even get to the second cognition, it is equally as hard to learn the ropes operating under this new system of cognition.

At the outset, none of us have a keen sense of discernment. We are either too gullible and accept things at face value, or we are too skeptical and deny what our intuition tells us because it conflicts with what we have known to that point in our lives. Discernment comes when we can strike the balance between these two polarities. Don't be so gullible to just accept everything, and don't be too cynical to automatically reject what your new awareness presents to you in the way of information. There is nothing wrong with healthy skepticism, so long as you don't let that skepticism turn into automatic denial because the information conflicts with what you think you know.

Don Juan taught that a spiritual warrior is nothing if not pragmatic. You have to be pragmatic in your ventures into higher cognitive awareness. There is no room for fancy or flightiness in the universe. There is no room in the second cognition for flakey people. If you are flakey, you won't get there to begin with, so not to worry.

I am telling you these things as a precursor to understanding the higher level of cognitive awareness. None of this is to tease you or frighten you; it is simply being pragmatic and telling you the truth of what to anticipate to a certain degree. You are going to have to start working on your discernment as you move yourself forward into the second cognition. The middle road between gullibility and skepticism can be found as you research to undo the perceptual misconceptions your awareness currently embraces. Start honing your skills to determine what is right and what is hogwash by using critical thinking coupled with what some call gut instinct. Pay attention to your gut reaction to things and rely more on that than on thinking, for gut reaction is a form of intuitive reckoning. It is through weighing what you find with what you know that you start to develop your own intuitive skills and your discernment.

I find that most people on a spiritual quest are less interested in doing the required work than they are in chasing flights of fancy from their ego desires. If you are content to continually seek butterflies and rainbows, then you will never find the second cognition. The pursuit of the second cognition is not for the weekend warriors of the spiritual community. It takes dedication. One has to live, breathe and eat spirit if they have any hope of advancing their cognitive awareness. You must have a will to power. This will not be achieved by laziness, nor will it be achieved by those who have adopted spiritual pursuit as a group social gathering. The second cognition will not be found in a group setting, it is not a Sunday social.

8

Your Personal Path and Why it is Personal

There is a lot of material in the spiritual arena that truthfully tells people that the spirit path, the path to higher cognitive awareness, is a personal journey. What is rarely mentioned is exactly *why* this is true. The main reason that the road to your own cognitive advancement is personal is that, even if we are all controlled by the ego's programming, how the ego has shaped each of us is on an individual basis.

No two people on the planet have the exact same experiences that shape their emotional dispositions. For the most part, everyone's emotional system of interpretation is predicated on the ego. In turn, the ego is shaped in large part by our environments as we move through life. How we were raised, what the home environment was, whether we are a child brought up in a war-torn country or a broken home, whether we are raised in comfort or poverty - each of these factors are issues that shape our individual egos. Alongside of these environmental nurturing issues we also have the individual issue of how we each deal with any given emotionally traumatic circumstance in our lives. Some people deal with mental stress better than others. Some people are mentally stronger and can deal with more stressful situations better than others. All of these factors combine to make each of us unique in the composition of our individual psyches. For this reason, there is no 'group' solution to advancing into the second cognition. There is no 'one size fits all' solution to advancing your own cognitive awareness.

In time, I can see the possibility of a broader means of teaching people in the second system of cognitive awareness when enough have crossed that threshold to serve as an alternative example for the second cognition, but with the world as it currently operates under tremendous ego control and cultural pressures, the path to advanced cognitive awareness must be a personal journey.

How fast anyone advances is determined by their own will to power, their own keen desire to succeed, and their battle against their own ego and its perceptions in the first cognition. It seems to be human nature to embrace what is known, because what is known is comfortable. Our societies, simply being magnified aspects of the ego in general, work against each and every person who seeks to advance their own consciousness. Ego enculturation keeps itself in place through peer pressure, criticism and scorn for anything or anyone who doesn't fit the cultural definition of 'normal'. Many people do not have the strength to go against this mental tide of the system of ego control which rules the first cognition. This is another key reason that the path to the second cognition is so difficult.

All our lives we have been taught to fit in, to not go against the accepted cultural boundaries of our societies. It is this ingrained ego need to fit in that works against every individual who is seeking to escape that mental prison. Most people fear to literally walk alone in the world, yet at this time in our conscious evolution, this is a requirement of moving into the second cognition. If you can't live with the fact that as you develop your cognitive abilities, that you will find yourself farther and farther removed than those around you in the sense of your cognitive advancement, then the path to the second cognition will be nigh unto impossible to attain.

The ego loves company; that is why it continually seeks like-minded people with which to associate. There is mental comfort in the ego need to fit in where the first cognition is concerned. As we were growing up, many of us were scorned as the outsider to certain circles in school. This type of being ostracized is nothing but a reinforcement tool of petty ego minds to set themselves up as better than others. Such habits are exhibited in children and they follow us into adulthood. It is all nothing more than ego enculturation continually reproducing itself, just as Nietzsche related.

As you move toward more cognitive advancement, even amongst like-minded friends you may associate with in the spiritual community, you are eventually going to find yourself at odds with those who have embraced the mystical form of wishful-thinking spiritualism, for truth has no place in their world of mystical fantasy. As I said, to advance into the second cognition, one has to be extremely pragmatic. You will find little pragmatism with people who keep buying pie in the sky illusions of what they think the spirit path is all about. If you stay your course, you are going to find yourself turning more and more serious in what you seek as well as what is revealed to you as you undo the ego illusions of reality. Trying to relate such pragmatic findings to your spiritual friends will usually result in you being accused of being too negative and they will eventually shun you. There is nothing negative about pragmatism or truth, although to those who embrace the fanciful notions of false spiritual understanding in the pop New Age culture, you will soon find all your presumed spiritual friends falling away as they continue on their path of chasing butterflies and rainbows while you continue to pursue truth. The same applies to those who are bound within a community of religious beliefs.

To move into the next level of cognitive awareness, you have to peel back the layers of an onion-like set of presumed truths and illusions. The more you dig into this research, the more troubled you will become, for you are on the path to discovering truth. You will have gained the wisdom to know that what is presented to the world defined as reality is nothing more than a vast and dreadful perceptual illusion. When you realize this, you are going to experience a serious bout of cognitive dissonance. You will have to face the truth that virtually everything you think you know is false, and that is a huge pill for anyone to swallow. You are going to have to find the strength within you to persevere in the face of these revelations if you hold any chance for success.

So now you have to ask yourself how many of your presumed spiritual teachers have told you these truths? How many have told you, in all their books and seminars that the path is as hard as what has been described in this book? And if they haven't told you, you must ask yourself if they are as much a spiritual expert as you once presumed?

The New Age culture is smothered in doctrinal passivity. It preaches love and light and thrives on group hugs and smiley faces. It is nothing more than a club of ego-driven people looking to fit in while claiming they are on the spirit path. Few of them have any real understanding about matters of spirit, or even what spirit means in that regard. They are virtually all hooked on the myths of the supernatural, mystical or magical. They are buying dreams into a realm that does not and never has existed except in the limited consciousness of the first cognition. They are seeking perpetual happiness as happiness is measured by the first cognition. Many believe in that concept of oneness, yet they are separated within themselves between the first cognition of the ego and what their own internal spirit can lead them to in the second cognition. If you look at it, it is just as Nietzsche portrayed - they are a rope between ape and the overman.

What I am sharing here is not a polemic any more than Nietzsche when he composed *The Antichrist.* These are simply truthful observations from the point of the second cognition. The question you must ask yourself, if you happen to be into the New Age form of spirituality, is whether you can face the truth, or if you are simply another defender of the first cognition with its superficial system of beliefs? Do you have the personal will to power to see the illusion for what it is and advance away from it through your own pragmatic process of willful evolution to become a self-created consciousness? *This* is the spirit path, *this* is the will to power, *this* is the requirement to attain the second cognition - *this* is the truth!

It doesn't matter what form of first cognition belief system you adhere to, for all of them are based in perceptual illusion. Whether you believe in supernatural gods or hard material science, you are still operating under a limited illusion that blinds you to a greater reality. Material science is in the business of quantifying and measuring everything. Its focus is on repeatable experimentation and all of its measure is strictly from the empiricist perspective of the material world. If something doesn't show itself in the material perception, it doesn't exist or is considered to be supernatural superstition. Staunch material scientists can't even accept what quantum theory is starting to open up where something more than the material world exhibits itself through mathematical equations. If the materialists can't even give a nod to the quantum physicists, how far do you think they will go in accepting what is presented with the information in this book?

Scientists are just as limited and hampered in their perceptual beliefs as any religionist or rainbow-chasing spiritualist of any kind. No matter which way you turn as you advance into the second cognition, you will be met with scorn and ridicule. Science and Atheism are basically the religions of the non-religious.

In order to move into advanced cognitive awareness, based on our current systems of reckoning, you are going to require information. You have to develop the skill and discernment to digest information without placing those who provide the information on the pedestal of authority. Searching for information is going to take you a long while on your path to unraveling your own personal illusions. At some point you are going to discover that much of the information you are seeking just plain runs out. You will find there is no place to turn for new input, and that is the point where you just have to start figuring things out for yourself.

All along the way, you are going to be facing varying levels of cognitive dissonance as your personal world of perceived illusions starts to crumble. Sometimes they may be minor, and other times they will be very overpowering revelations. Your intuitive skills will start to develop during this stage of unraveling your own personal perceptions of reality. The intuitive side of yourself, given the proper nourishment, will give you the ability to read between the lines of much of the information and disinformation presented and you will see stories only partially told by historians and news reporters. I encourage you to develop these intuitive skills for they are going to be your guide to understanding in the second cognition.

Everyone has intuition but very few people pay attention to it. It is a latent part of our cognitive abilities that our societies put no educational emphasis on in the public forum for people to even know they have intuitive abilities that can be developed. Intuition is gravely overlooked in the first cognition and you will be hard pressed to find any real cogent studies into intuitive awareness, yet as you move into the second cognition, you are going to have to learn to rely on your intuitive skills to continue to advance your cognitive awareness, especially after the door to it opens for you.

9

Knowledge versus Understanding

We now come to the crux of this study. All the necessary explanations have been given as to what a shift in consciousness truly entails. In the world of the first cognition, knowledge is supreme, yet knowledge without understanding is useless. How many of you have been seeking the knowledge about consciousness, the knowledge about spirit? How many people worldwide profess to share such knowledge? How many people can remotely comprehend what is sold or interpreted as knowledge about cognitive awareness?

Multitudes of people have spiritual 'knowledge'. They have memorized and adopted all the doctrines their egos will embrace. They can recite chapter and verse about their knowledge on matters of spirit. But how many of them truly *understand* the knowledge they profess?

The fact is that knowledge, as it is currently understood in the first system of cognition, is merely an inventory of facts that we embrace and accept as reality. The vast majority of people seeking to understand consciousness are working from a stepping stone rather than using the ladder required to reach the heights of understanding. All the knowledge they possess in reference to consciousness is absolutely useless without the cognitive awareness to comprehend and understand what they think they know. The manner of interpreting cognitive awareness by those studying it in the first cognition is little different than watching travel shows on television and trying to state you understand the location simply by viewing it remotely.

At this point in human cognitive studies, all the researchers, whether they are experimenting with and studying the mechanics of the human brain, or whether they are psychologists or scientific philosophers pursuing knowledge about consciousness, are outsiders trying to see into a world they currently lack the cognitive ability to understand. They are all speculators. They theorize and they guess and they put forth profound sounding ideas about what they *think* expanded awareness is, but none of them has the inside scoop. None of them have experienced the second level of cognitive awareness as a constant lifestyle, and in that regard, they are all wandering around in the dark trying to comprehend what their cognitive system is not geared to perceive.

The road to advanced cognitive awareness has always been available, but the messengers of the truth have been shouted down by the evangelists of the material world of 3D matter and those who can't survive without mentally embracing some form of supernatural intervening force in their lives as an explanation. All the presumed knowledge the experts possess is not worth a whit without that ounce of understanding required to see something more. The expounders of knowledge have no understanding of what they seek, no matter how many ways the truth has been revealed to them to date. The interpretive circuitry of the ego cognition can *not* understand what real power is without corrupting it with the idea of a powerful ego.

What we call spirit has nothing to do with mysticism, nor does it have anything to do with the supernatural. Spirit is simply a word, a definition whose meaning has been misinterpreted over and over again. As Don Juan taught, we live in a world of definitions, of descriptions. To move into understanding spirit, which is actually nothing more than advanced cognitive awareness, we have to leave our world of definitions behind. One can't describe the wisdom provided by intuitive knowing. One can't describe either the mechanics or the method through which it works. It can't be defined, it can only be experienced. Our system of language is hopelessly insufficient to describe the second level of cognitive awareness, and that is why I am not trying to describe it for the reader. I'm only here to tell you that the second cognition exists and have explained the trials and tribulations one must face to get there.

Where the second level of cognitive awareness is concerned - spirit - you can't understand spirit (the second cognition) until you experience it, and only through having experienced it as a way of being, as part of your daily life, will you understand it. I can give no explanation to your world of definitions of exactly what it is other than to tell you that it is there and it is attainable. How does one describe the indescribable? All we can do is use allegory to try and explain to the limited cognition of the first awareness what the second cognition opens up for you.

I have had to use allegory to explain many of the principles of the second cognition throughout this book. Through the use of modern vernacular, I have worked to reveal the meaning of others who used allegories in the past to try and explain the same things throughout the ages, although their manner was often less direct than this presentation. This work is a study of clarification. I have done my best to remove any and all hints of the supernatural in this presentation and lay the foundation for understanding the existence of the second form of cognitive awareness available to humanity. I have explained what a shift in consciousness not only takes us away from, but also where the shift is geared to take us forward. In retrospect, I don't see how the principle could be more precisely revealed, nor more cogently explained than this bare bones presentation of no nonsense facts.

Who I am is not important. The greater importance lies in discovering who you really are under the tyranny of the ego lies and presumed perceptions that you call reality. I will not set myself up to be pilloried or vilified by the detractors living under the spell of the first cognition. I will not go the way of my scorned predecessors into heightened awareness, for it is unnecessary. I will not become the next guru for I do not want a following nor do I desire fame or public acclaim. It is as Nietzsche said, I want people *"who will follow me because they want to follow themselves."* To achieve your own shift in cognitive awareness you need to follow yourself. I have provided the material you need to guide you on your own road, so I suggest you take on the task and do it for yourself. I have done my part in providing you the knowledge you need to progress forward. It is up to you to find your own understanding. That is the path of willful evolution. That is the path to becoming a self-created consciousness. I wish you the best on your journey.

REFERENCES

Festinger, Leon - *The Theory of Cognitive Dissonance,* 1957, *Stanford University Press*

Nietzsche, Friedrich - *Thus Spake Zarathustra*, 1883 - Public Domain

Nietzsche, Friedrich - *The Antichrist,* 1895, Public Domain

Nietzsche, Friedrich - *The Will to Power,* 1901, Public Domain

Castenada, Carlos - *The Teachings of don Juan; A Separate Reality; Journey to Ixtlan; Tales of Power; The Second Ring of Power; The Eagle's Gift; The Fire From Within; The Power of Silence; The Art of Dreaming; The Active Side of Infinity,* Washington Square Press, 1968-1998

Jesus - *The Gospel of Thomas,* Translation by Messrs. Brill of Lieden; *The Holy Bible*, New Testament quotes.

ABOUT THE AUTHOR

Who the author of this book is matters less to the reader than discovering who you are. The author is just a human being who has moved into the different state of consciousness awareness explained in this book - the same state of conscious awareness open to every human being who will search to find it.

INDEX

www.ingramcontent.com/pod-product-compliance
Lightning Source LLC
Chambersburg PA
CBHW070929290526
45795CB00001B/478